The Urbana Free Library

To renew: call 217-367-4057
or go to "*urbanafreelibrary.org*"
and select "Renew/Request Items"

OUTSIDE THE WIRE

THERE IS NO
GREATER AGONY
THAN BEARING
AN UNTOLD STORY
INSIDE YOU.

—MAYA ANGELOU

OUTSIDE THE WIRE

American Soldiers' Voices from Afghanistan

EDITED BY CHRISTINE DUMAINE LECHE

FOREWORD BY BRIAN TURNER

UNIVERSITY OF VIRGINIA PRESS   CHARLOTTESVILLE AND LONDON

University of Virginia Press
© 2013 by the Rector and Visitors of the University of Virginia
All rights reserved
Printed in the United States of America on acid-free paper

First published 2013

9 8 7 6 5 4 3 2 1

Library of Congress Cataloging-in-Publication Data

Outside the wire : American soldiers' voices from Afghanistan / edited by
Christine Dumaine Leche ; foreword by Brian Turner.
       pages   cm
   Includes bibliographical references.
    ISBN 978-0-8139-3411-2 (cloth : alk. paper)—ISBN 978-0-8139-3412-9
(e-book)
    1. Afghan War, 2001—Personal narratives, American. 2. United
States—Armed Forces—Military life—Anecdotes. 3. United States—
Armed Forces—Biography—Anecdotes. 4. Soldiers' writings, American.
I. Leche, Christine Dumaine, 1949–
    DS371.413.095 2013
    958.104'74092273—dc23

                                                    2012044554

For the American men and women, and their families,
who bear the weight of war for us all

Contents

Foreword

Histories are too often told from the vantage point of power—from the courtly heights of kings, queens, and emperors; through the map-maker's scope during a sultan's rule; influenced by the diplomatic pressures and nuances of a president's years in office. The problem with these versions of history is that they function more like sketches, or outlines. History rings truer to my ear when it is spoken from the pavement of the street, the kitchen table, the local grocery store. How much was a gallon of milk? What did the old men and women say when they looked up from the daily paper and added their own corrections to the print? What did people say at the bus stop once the rain let up? What did friends, family, and lovers say to one another when they finally shared the things that kept them up late at night? These are the voices of history.

And these are the voices in *Outside the Wire*. The nonfiction pieces included here offer us that rare opportunity to learn history from some of those who took part in it, lived it, experienced it. This is no simple matter. I often hear civilians lament that so many veterans keep their experiences to themselves. In my own family, I have to admit, none of the veterans spoke to me of war until I returned from one. They told me a great many things about war and wartime experience, but always in stories that circled around or remained on the periphery of actual combat experience.

Many soldiers place their experiences in a box and bury it down inside them, and if they do share from it once they return home, rarely do they speak of these experiences with those who aren't veterans of combat zones themselves. The veteran and the civilian become alienated from one another over a widening gulf of silence. What may seem curiosity in nonveterans may be interpreted by veterans as a voyeuristic desire to "overhear" the sounds of battle, the din of war, the obscene and the horrific. Meanwhile, often nonveterans worry that asking veterans to share their experiences can seem like asking someone to twist a knife buried deep within—to ask the veteran to bleed just so the outsider might better comprehend the warrior who's returned home.

It's important to hear these experiences, I believe, because it can help the nonveteran better understand those who serve in uniform. The anonymity that the uniform provides serves to strip away the individuality of the person wearing it, at least from an outsider's perspective. The definition of the word *uniform* is instructive here: always the same; unvarying. And once in uniform, the warrior assumes a name that resides outside of civilian experience. (Letitia Hernandez becomes LT Hernandez, for example.) I encourage the reader to discover the humanity of the person whose warrior name and uniform separate him or her from the wider culture. In literary theory circles, one of the dominant modes of the past twenty years has been the recognition of the "other," with a subsequent intent of breaking down the stereotypes that construct the "other" so that the *others* might regain their individual humanity. *Outside the Wire* is involved in this very process.

For those who've served in uniform, I encourage you to read this book, too. In these pages you'll hear voices that might take you back to your own time in service. The adrenaline, the boredom, the laughter—a wide range of experience is gathered together here. In fact, that's one of the virtues of this collection: It is an accumulation of the voices and experiences of many veterans and service members (as well as of voices from the home front), which combine to offer us a wide landscape during a particular time in history. I have never been to Afghanistan, for example, but through the aggregate of these individual voices I get a sense of what it might be like for those serving in uniform there. These voices are different from those of soldiers I served with, but in them I recognize many of the men and women I served with during my own time in uniform.

It is difficult to imagine how the writers in *Outside the Wire* were able even to put pen to paper, given the circumstances. And much of the writing here has a rough quality to it. But there is a real virtue in this. Give me the unvarnished. Varnish conceals the blemish, and the blemish is part of the story carried in the grain of the wood. My own poems, written while I was in Iraq from 2003 to 2004, share many similarities with the pieces gathered in this book. I value the "rough" quality of the words I wrote then because the language we choose under duress speaks volumes to the moment we are living. If these writers live long enough, and if they choose one day to do so, they may later write down that which they have gained through recollection and in (relative) tranquility. Distance and perspective offer the possibility of great insight, it's true. Still, there is so much to be learned from language that crackles with the immediacy of the experience.

Before I step aside here so that the reader can turn to the pages these men and women have brought to this book, I'd like to commend Chris Leche for nurturing this project and seeing it through to publication. Chris crossed the line of departure and entered a combat zone so that she might help service members achieve their educational goals. And she became a mentor to men and women who would serve, through language, as writers of witness, to those who transformed experience so that it might be shared with us, here, at home. When I imagine Chris teaching the fundamentals of the narrative essay to service members in a FOB or on a remote base near the border with Pakistan, the word *absurd* comes to mind. It seems impossible. And yet this is exactly what she volunteered to do (and more, in fact). What Chris has done in many ways exemplifies what truly sane people are capable of achieving in an often absurd and difficult world.

Brian Turner
June 26, 2011

Soldier-poet Brian Turner is the author of two books of poetry: *Here, Bullet* (2005), a *New York Times* Editors' Choice selection, and *Phantom Noise* (2010). He is the author of the poem "The Hurt Locker," from which the 2008 film took its title. Brian Turner served as an infantry team leader in Iraq with the 3rd Stryker Brigade Combat Team, 2nd Infantry Division, from 2003 to 2004.

Preface

The e-mail at the top of my Yahoo list read, "Doc, sorry I couldn't make it to class last night, but with the suicide bomber and everything, I was kept really busy. Can you send the assignment?" I assured my student that our English 101 class had been canceled. In fact, on the evening of the suicide bomber scare on Bagram Air Base in Afghanistan, I had sequestered myself in my 6 x 10–foot sleeping quarters in a plywood B-hut (a semi-permanent wooden structure used as a replacement for a tent, which housed six to eight soldiers and civilians). The civilians working in the camp had not been immediately alerted to the "situation." We surmised there might be a problem when the camp first turned eerily quiet and soon afterward became frenetic with the pounding of boots on cement and gravel. There were no other sounds—no shouts, no whispers. Every soldier was executing his or her mission, each wearing a flak vest and a Kevlar helmet and grasping an M16 at the ready. Meanwhile, civilians like me hurried to our unprotected B-huts. We closed the door behind us, locking ourselves in with a flimsy screen-door latch.

I can only describe as fate the turn of events that led to my teaching for the University of Maryland University College Europe and to a passion for teaching soldiers and veterans. As a forty-six-year-old with a new PhD in hand, I had intended to teach as an adjunct while applying for tenure-track positions. Then my husband, Jacques, called from work one day. "Listen," he said, "the military is looking for a pharmacist in Germany. What would you think of just selling the house and moving?"

The logistics fell into place. In researching teaching possibilities I came across UMUC Europe's program for military members and spouses, contacted the Academic Director for English, and was soon assigned a couple of classes on an American military base in Kirch-Göns, Germany. Fine, good enough, but what I most wanted was a full-time position. I again contacted the Academic Director. "Sure," he said. "You can teach for us full-time. Would you be willing to go to combat training in Hohenfels, Germany, and then on to

Bosnia in a couple of weeks?" The Dayton Agreement, which ended the Bosnian conflict, had been signed only a couple of months before, so for the first time since the Vietnam War, UMUC Europe would be sending faculty to a war zone. I could hear the sneer in the Director's laugh on the other end of the line stop short when I said, "Yes, absolutely." No one in my family had ever been in the military. I lacked a personal cause. But in a moment of epiphany, my path was clear.

Following the signing of the Dayton Agreement ending the Bosnian conflict, I had the honor of teaching soldiers deployed to Bosnia. I taught, in American military camps, courses in English, literature, creative writing, and speech for UMUC Europe, which has held the contract for classes in active war zones for several decades. In fact, for the next three years I rotated between teaching soldiers deployed to camps in Bosnia and teaching those assigned to bases in Germany. I also taught active-duty soldiers deployed to Camp Bondsteel, Kosovo, following the Kosovo conflict. In 2002 I assumed the position of Academic Director for English, Communications, and Foreign Languages for UMUC Europe, which meant I lived and worked in the university's office in Heidelberg, Germany. I held this position for several years before my husband and I decided to return to the States—specifically, to Austin, Texas. Once settled, I resumed teaching active-duty soldiers and veterans, only now online from the comfort of my suburban study. But I missed the interaction of the live classroom, and I missed teaching deployed soldiers. I soon volunteered to teach in military camps in Afghanistan—both on Bagram Air Base and on a FOB (acronym for forward operating base, pronounced "fob") near the Pakistan border. I knew there would be plenty of students, since deployed soldiers take classes because they are working on a degree, need a diversion from the military, or are earning college credit in order to move up in rank.

On Bagram Air Base we sat together in cement classrooms in a building left over from the Soviet occupation of the 1970s. None of the windows opened in the old stucco rooms, so in summer we worked in 117-degree heat. We also met in B-huts, bunkers, a chapel, and in the corner of a dining hall. We sat in a circle on the yellow plastic floor of an empty tent under bare lightbulbs. During one evening of good luck, we luxuriated in padded swivel chairs around a long mahogany table in the TACC (tactical air command center). That heavenly room, which was on very short loan, came with a projector, sound system, illuminated maps of Afghanistan, and a refrigerator stocked with bottled water. In that room a young female private called me over before class to explain why she had been absent the previous week. She had been sent to a FOB, and in attempting to return for class had caught a ride in a convoy of Humvees that would take her to yet another FOB where she might hitch a flight on a helicopter back to Bagram. The unforgettable story of her journey is related in "They Were Just Kids."

Student-soldiers attended class after eighteen hours of guard duty, after cleaning human remains from medevac (medical evacuation) helicopters, after all-day patrols outside the safety of the concertina wire surrounding the camp, after washing bodies in the morgue, after having been raped by a fellow soldier in the camp a week earlier, after defusing IEDs (improvised explosive devices), after watching their wives give birth via Skype, and after working with a surgeon for hours to save the lives of two seventeen-year-old Afghani boys whose legs had been severed when they drove over an IED returning home from a New Year's Eve party. In this last case, my student, a military nurse, rushed into English class late, the impression from the netting of the surgical mask still marking her face.

It was in FOB Salerno before the start of class one evening that a lanky infantry soldier from Missouri, still jittery from a firefight a few hours earlier, yelled out, "Want to see how I shot that haji who was taking potshots at me, Doc?" He was standing behind his chair as he pressed his hands together; his forefingers became the muzzle of a gun held at his waist. He buckled his knees and sprayed the classroom with invisible bullets side to side: boom, boom, boom. "It was me or him, and I ain't proud but I damn as hell lived!" Then he sat at a table and pulled out a working draft of his creative writing assignment. The Afghan dirt still under his fingernails was a metaphor for the emotional residue of his day, the traces of which might take years to dislodge. Sometimes the students came to class traumatized, yes, but also ready for a break from the burdens of military life. More often than not, they were ready to write.

On a deeply personal level, each soldier must confront the paradox that love of country and hatred of those who would threaten its peace sometimes lead to violence on a grand scale. War is a skewering of peacetime morals. Specialist Andrew Stock, a student in Afghanistan, says in his memoir "The Hate" that he keeps a bracelet with the Sanskrit mantra *Om mani padme hum* (the mantra of the bodhisattva of compassion) on the stock of his machine gun, and the irony of that action does not escape him. Many of our men and women return from war suffering from PTSD (Post-Traumatic Stress Disorder) as a result of the emotional dissonance described so well by Sergeant Stock. Over and over, soldiers talked or wrote about war-zone experiences that challenged their civilian concept of morality. Yet they had chosen war as a vocation, one that distances them physically and psychologically from those they love back home.

To include yet another example of the contradictions of war: One night a twenty-year-old soldier in English 101 offered to read her homework assignment to the class. She was sitting at a long table with several other students and was dressed in a navy-blue-and-gray Air Force PT (physical training) uniform. The crisp nylon jacket crinkled as her trembling hand lifted the sheet of white paper and she described a frantic scene at Bagram Air Base hospital, where she worked as a medic. Two medevac helicopters had brought in several wounded American soldiers along with the equally injured insurgents who had shot them. One of the Americans soon died, and my student was ordered to clean his body. Hours later, an insurgent coded—his heart stopped as he lay in a hospital bed. Her orders now were to give the chest compressions that would save his life. Was he the insurgent who had killed the American soldier? She laid her head on the desk and cried in deep, guttural sobs.

Sergeant Stock wonders if he can remain compassionate about his fellow soldiers and humankind and at the same time engage in combat. In creative writing classes in Afghanistan, soldiers wrote to ease the uncertainty and the loneliness of the moment. They wrote memoirs, poems, monologues, and brief plays. Some wrote about recent combat experiences, perhaps as a way of exploring their literal and psychological reactions throughout or after the event. Others focused on moments that occurred during earlier deployments to Iraq or Afghanistan, ones they had processed or had gained enough distance from to explore further and to share. Others wrote about some aspect of deployment, such as what it feels like to embark on a dangerous mission, or about the often repetitive days in a military camp. Still others relived the terror of rocket and mortar attacks. A few chose to skip writing about war altogether and mined the vast territory of childhood or adolescence for material. The range of their experiences and concerns is represented in this collection as soldiers "speak" directly to the reader about the details of their lives on and off the battlefield.

The soldiers in my classes contributed their writings only after the semester ended. Until then, they were unaware their stories might be included in a book. In fact, I only thought of the idea myself after I had been teaching in Afghanistan several months. I was awed by the men and women I met—by their endurance, patience, honor, judgment, and the humor with which they balanced day-to-day hardship. After class they might head off to twelve hours of guard duty in a cold wooden tower overlooking the blackness of the Afghan countryside, or back to the flight line to work all night replacing worn parts in a helicopter engine, or to the dining hall to help prepare the midnight meal for pilots flying late-night bombing missions. I was struck by the determination of my soldier-students and by the realization that so few Americans know the life of an American soldier.

Our soldiers carry the weight of war for each of us. This book is about giving voice to the dedicated, talented, unassuming people I've had the honor of working with in many classes throughout the years. Although the particular voices collected here are those of soldiers deployed to Afghanistan, they speak for all American soldiers for all time. Soldiers are all too often stereotyped. We may as a culture *honor* them, but most of us don't *know* them, and this book is about creating connection. I hope that I have furthered this cause by including both combat pieces and childhood reflections and memories, because life in a war zone is punctuated almost equally by feelings of intense fear and nostalgic memories from the past (often childhood) or present (back home). The organization of the writings in this collection imitates the leaps the soldier's mind makes across continents and decades.

During my time in Afghanistan, I experienced my share of mortar and rocket attacks, all-night waits in the cold PAX (military passenger terminal), and flights on small, vulnerable planes. But one evening after teaching a class on FOB Salerno, I felt for a few moments like a real soldier. My class had ended with the usual shuffle

A few members of a creative writing class on Bagram Air Base. *Clockwise from top left:* SGT John Wisnofsky, SFC Evelyn Matheny, Christine Leche, SGT Danielle Dumas, SSgt Nathan Dooge, PFC Iman Chin, and SGT Jessie Evans showing off his muscles for the camera. (Courtesy of Nichole Healy)

of papers, the battle-rattle of M16s, and the thudding of eighteen pairs of desert boots leaving the room. The space designated for class that evening was a small free-standing building called "The Lodge," complete with external laminate paneling that mimicked split logs. And according to our map, this cozy log cabin was snuggled close to the Pakistan border in Khost Province in southeastern Afghanistan, a Taliban stronghold.

Salerno is a blackout camp for security reasons, so before I left the classroom I slipped my microlight, a thumb-sized LED device that I used to throw a thin line of strobe light onto my feet, out from my coat pocket and switched off the fluorescent lights in the room. I heard the door click shut and lock behind me and was swallowed into the mouth of thick Afghan darkness.

After only a few feet I could see no trace of the building I had just stepped out of. Nor could I see the fat ring of concertina wire that held us safely inside the perimeter. Equally invisible was my hand held directly in front of my eyes unless I shined the green strobe across my fingers. I was quickly disoriented.

My English class usually met in a building closer to the center of the camp, near the gym and the dining hall. On these occasions when I closed the classroom door, even if I was unable to see an actual walking body, I could make out tiny points of green light moving within the main square. I had learned the general direction of the gym, the latrine, and my room. Because of the high rate of incoming mortars and rockets, all barracks were built as bunkers with foot-thick ceilings and walls. I thought of the safety of this building as "home."

But that night in the cave-like blackness, I eased each foot forward an inch at a time and stretched my arms out in space hoping one of them would touch the edge of a building. I thought of Edgar Allan Poe's "The Cast of Amontillado" and the terrible darkness that Fortunato must have endured within the tombed walls. My heart raced. I thought of God—Let there be light, and there was light, but not in the heart of this war-ravaged land. I feebly stepped forward, remembering the people in my life who have sought out the wilderness in order to count the stars. I wanted to ask, but what if the clouds roll in and your flashlight dies and your cell phone is out of range?

My outstretched hand struck a tree trunk, and then another and another, and I knew I was on the deserted edge of camp along a peach orchard that once belonged to an Afghan farmer. I knew I must be within the camp, but because I could not see the concertina wire, I still feared I was in the open countryside in a swarm of impending insurgents. "Go by the way of not knowing." I settled on this Zen maxim, which I repeated like the beat of a drum.

Then over my head came the soft swoosh, swoosh of mortar rounds, followed by explosions. I thought they might be coming from the west, given the position of the peach orchard, but the terrain was hilly, so although the ground vibrated with each hit, I could not see the explosions. I stopped. Keep moving, I told myself. Suddenly I heard what seemed to be a platoon of feet patting the rutted dirt path.

Up close, I heard men talking low in Pashto and walking fast. I held my green strobe out and caught a vague shadow of white tunics and swaying pants only inches away. I pictured the battered Nike or Adidas sport shoes they all seem to wear, gray with dirt and lacking shoelaces, which is why they make that flip-flop noise with each step. LNs (local nationals) worked in the camp, cleaning showers and toilets, mopping floors, and digging ditches. They would have an English-speaking guard, probably an American. I thought of calling out but hesitated. Suppose I had somehow wandered outside the wire? By then they had already sunk into the night. I continued to inch forward.

It wasn't long before I heard a male voice say in a deep midwestern drawl, "Who's out there? I hear somebody out there." Then more demanding: "Identify yourself." A green speck of light caught my eye, and I saw that the wrist holding it was wearing US Army desert camouflage. I would later learn he was Sergeant Barry Williams from Dayton, Ohio. I was safe.

"Go by the way of not knowing." How frightened I had been. And then it struck me that our soldiers do exactly this for all of us every single day at war. They always have. And they will tell you that they always will.

Christine Dumaine Leche
September 15, 2011
Austin, Texas

Acknowledgments

With gratitude to the soldiers who were students in my creative writing and English classes in Afghanistan. We shared difficult living conditions, rocket and mortar attacks, and small planes. I felt honored to work with each of you. You protect us all. I will always remember.

With love and thanks to my husband, Jacques, who believes in my passion for teaching soldiers wherever they happen to be deployed and who makes me feel that dreams are possibilities and then supports me as I live them. It's been (and remains) a great ride, honey.

I would like to say thank you to the University of Maryland University College Europe. UMUC began offering face-to-face courses to soldiers in 1949, followed soldiers to Vietnam, and has since provided education to soldiers and veterans throughout the world, both in war zones and on bases in Europe, Asia, and other parts of the globe. I bow deeply to your program.

I would not have been able to complete this project without the continual support and remarkable vision of Cathie Brettschneider, Acquisitions Editor for Humanities at UVa Press. None finer. Your passion for this anthology, your commitment to the soldiers' words, kept me inspired along the way. No doubt our collaboration was meant to be. Enormous thanks as well to Ellen Satrom, Managing Editor, also of UVa Press, whose fine, artistic eye brought the language in much of my own writing into tighter focus. You always knew what I intended to say. Your praise of this project gives me joy.

Thanks to Austin Community College Dean of Communications, Hazel Ward, Dean of Arts and Humanities, Lyman Grant, and Department Chair of Creative Writing, Charlotte Gullick, all of whom saw the need for veterans-only courses, made them happen, and asked that I teach them.

With gratitude to 2nd Lieutenant Kelly Singleton Dalton, helicopter pilot in the Second Gulf War and author of a remarkable thesis submitted in 2010 in completion of a master of arts degree from Georgetown University titled "From Combat to Composition: Meeting the Needs of Military Veterans through Postsecondary Writing Pedagogy." Kelly, you both lived the soldiers' military and academic experiences and then cogently and passionately enlightened the rest of us. My understanding of the issues veterans face as returning students comes, in part, from you. Sincere thanks.

The following family members and close friends were with me every step of this project. You were patient in listening to my fears, but like the best of friends, you nudged me ever closer to my dream: Blake Leche, Heather Montgomery, Mandi Leche, Mike Montgomery, Dorothy Barnett, Joann Cohn, Jack Getman, Diane Gregg, Keith Kesler, and Terri Leclerq. Each of you is an inspiration, and I love you.

OUTSIDE THE WIRE

SPRING I sit on a stone bench in Bayswater Park, Queens, in the oppressive July heat. The burned-earth odor of weed mixes with the smoke of dripping fat from the burgers on one of the public grills. A vagrant pisses on a tree trunk not twenty feet away. A few small children, seemingly alone, run in and out of the sprinklers, and older kids play homicide on the handball court. The scorching sun sears my face and arms. The recruiter next to me keeps talking, determined to persuade me to join the Army.

"Look around you," he says. "Is this really how you want to live?"

Homeless people wander aimlessly. Fifteen-year-old mothers push babies and toddlers back and forth in rusted grocery carts, back and forth, scanning the scene looking for a sucker to take care of their kids. The atmosphere is indeed glum.

Sergeant Smith, bald with thick eyebrows, maintains a pleasant smile. After a long silence, I turn to look him in the eyes, which hold a mysterious pain of their own. These eyes got my attention the first time we met: brown, lifeless pools that unnerved me yet were as familiar as the view of my neighborhood from my bedroom window. His are the same eyes plastered on the faces of my friends, the people in my community, and, sadly enough, my own in the mirror. I break the spell of his gaze long enough to answer his question.

"No," I say with hesitation. "I want more for myself." My stomach is a lump of anxiety weighted with guilt. I would be leaving my family in New York. To think of saying good-bye to my mom makes my veins feel frostbitten. I see her sweet face, the patient features that reflect my own. Will she resent me?

Sergeant Smith capitalizes on my hesitation. His voice swells with urgency. "The 'hood don't give a damn about you! There's no future for you out here! The Army can open a whole new world to you!"

His next words hit me like a bullet: "You don't want to end up

1

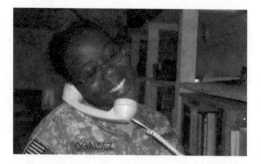

Specialist Chantal Ogaldez at work in the Technical Supply Office in an aviation hangar on Bagram Air Base, Afghanistan, June 2009. (Courtesy of Specialist Chantal Ogaldez)

like your family members, struggling to get by each and every day but not doing anything to change their lives."

This is true, I think. My cousin and her three children sleep on our floor because they have nowhere else to lay their heads. My aunt takes her grandkids to the hospital every few weeks to have the roaches pulled from their ears. My uncle drinks himself out of his mind.

I must make a move. I look at the scene in the park. Hopelessness and despair mixed with rage. In two months I am on my way to Fort Jackson for basic training.

Specialist Chantal Ogaldez, US Army, served in Afghanistan.
MOS: 92A Automated Logistical Specialist
HOMETOWN: Far Rockaway, New York

I have left the military and am now a certified medical assistant. I plan to pursue a career in nursing because I really love helping people.

DEPLOYMENT   My duffle bags lay clumped in the bed of my truck, and in the backseat all three of my boys were weeping as quietly as they could manage in order to spare me more of the wretched heartache that comes with leaving them behind for fifteen months. I was to drop off my bags at the two-tone military-tan building with the rusted window ledges where I usually worked. By the traffic jam in the parking lot, it was clear I would not be the only one who would be breaking down into tears. I pulled my bags from the truck bed and began placing them in the neat rows already begun by the several hundred others there, rows called "dress right dress." My oldest son, Austin, grabbed my duffle, which was just about as tall as he, and without uttering a word walked right by me and placed my bag in perfect unison with the others.

First Sergeant Alkire conducted roll call, the moment we had all been waiting for. We had already drawn our weapons and night-vision goggles, so we could now look for a place to be "alone" with our wives and children, parents, girlfriends, boyfriends—alone so we could cry. Lord knows soldiers can't cry in front of each other. I could already hear one of the guys popping off with, "Hey, Bobby, did you see Billy crying like a sissy so much he couldn't even kiss his wife good-bye?"

The dreaded time had come. Time to walk to the family truck and say good-bye. My wife, Stefanie, and I walked hand in hand. She was squeezing my hand pretty hard. The walk to the truck seemed like the "green mile." I picked up my two youngest, Devon and Caleb.

"Where are you going, Daddy?" asked Caleb.

"I'm going to Iraq to make it a better place."

Then he plunged his fist, a pretend dagger, into my heart. My oldest, Austin, assured me he would be the man of the house.

Then Caleb piped up again, "Are you going to die in Iraq, Daddy?" Before I could answer he started crying as if he had broken his leg—long, deep, guttural screams.

Devon, who has Down syndrome and is a total daddy's boy, said, "Daddy, no die please." He too began to cry hysterically.

Then I did something for which I would have punished my children. I lied to them. I said I was not going to die and would be home before they knew it. I watched the blue truck drive away, my family fade into the sunlight.

I did see them again. I was wounded in combat. Two of my soldiers and my platoon leader, Lieutenant Fritz, were killed in action. Private First Class Millican died saving my life. While I lay in the Baghdad hospital, I looped over in my head what I might have done to save my soldiers. I had to see my wife and children again. All I could think about was the attack and what my family would have gone through had I been killed. I decided to take R&R.

As the plane pulled into the Atlanta terminal, I noticed a fire truck on each side of the runway. They were shooting water cannons over the plane in an arch as a welcome home gesture. Hundreds of people were lined up just inside the terminal door clapping and cheering for me and the other returning soldiers. For a moment the burdens of this awful war lifted, and I felt at peace.

At the check-in counter for my connecting flight, I was told I would be the only soldier on the plane. The check-in clerk said there might be an open seat in first class and asked that I wait before boarding. But as she was making the final call, a man in a suit came running up to the counter. The clerk then asked if he would be willing to give up his first-class seat for an injured soldier. He could see I was in the military as I was wearing my ACUs (Army Combat Uniform). "Not for the damned Army. Hell, no!" he said. I told the clerk not to worry, that there was no need for her to get in trouble over something so small.

After getting off the plane in Dallas, my last layover, all I wanted to do was sit on the floor by myself and listen to my favorite Christian rock group, Third Day, on my iPod. It was then that a tall, elderly man in jeans and a T-shirt walked over to me. I really did not want any more insults, so when he asked if he could talk to me I politely declined, moved to another open space, sat down and leaned against the wall, and then turned my music back on. To my surprise, he followed. He asked again if he could talk to me. I didn't even stand when I said no. I was about to break down and bawl my eyes out.

Sergeant First Class Billy Wallace the day he deployed to Iraq as part of Operation Iraqi Freedom, September 2006. With him, from top left, clockwise: Austin, 10; Chris Cubel, 9 (wife Stefanie's brother); Devon, 8; and Caleb, 3. (Courtesy of Stefanie Wallace)

In a soft-spoken tone he asked if I was okay. Then he explained that he was a volunteer at the airport greeting soldiers as they came through. He offered me a Bible, but I told him I had two in my bag. He asked if I had a cross to wear around my neck. I said, "I'm afraid mine was lost in a firefight in Karbala, Iraq. I'll get a new one when I get home." He slipped his from around his neck. The cross, he said, was made by someone in his church. It is like none I have ever seen—three nails held together with blue wire. I still wear it every day.

After reading this I would like you to do something for me in the event you ever come across a soldier in the airport. Although there is no need to give up your seat, please be kind. Yes, as soldiers, we do kill enemy combatants, but, I assure you, we don't like it. We must live with the fact we have killed for the rest of our lives. Regardless of how cool some soldiers make it sound, we don't like killing. We never tell you that most of us take medication just to cope with the nightmares so we can get some sleep, or about the other pills we feel too embarrassed to mention. I'll tell you what those pills do. They keep us from destroying what's left of the relationship with our family, that is, what the military has not already torn apart by sending us away for twelve to eighteen months at a time every other year. I am not asking for sympathy. War is what we have chosen. But if you cannot say anything nice to a soldier, please keep your thoughts to yourself.

KARBALA, IRAQ January 20th, 2007. I had just finished my twelve-hour shift as the NCOIC (noncommissioned officer in charge) of the command room we had established at the Karbala police station. The room measured about 8 x 12 feet with a false window. The outside had been bricked over. I felt like I was in a jail cell, but with a door I could use whenever I wanted.

The evening was totally out of the ordinary for me. Earlier I had started an argument with my wife on Yahoo Voice for no good reason, and I called her back one more time to apologize. Normally, when I get off shift I remain in the command room, take off my boots, and flop down for a few hours. But that particular evening, after I called my wife I lay right down with my boots still on.

Within minutes I jumped off the cot to the pop poppop of shots from within the police building. I was fumbling to put on my IBA (Interceptor Body Armor) when a man wearing what we call a chocolate-chip DCU (Desert Camouflage Uniform) and Kevlar helmet and carrying a cocked AK-47 slammed open the door to our office. I recognized him not by his face and full beard but by his uniform, which was that of an Iraqi soldier. I figured he must have heard the shots and was coming to grab us to help them fight. He was standing in the doorway not two feet from me when he drew his weapon and took direct aim at my face.

Sergeant First Class Bennett, Private First Class Millican, Specialist Washburn, and a sergeant from the military police were all in the room with me. I dropped my IBA and threw the left side of my body against the door, but the barrel of the AK-47 was already wedged in the jamb. The insurgent fired blindly into the room. Bullets ricocheted from the walls, ceiling, and floor and pinged against the refrigerator. My head was next to the muzzle as each round blasted out of the barrel. Then the weapon slid away from the open crack in the door and I slammed it shut. For a split second, silence.

Then a succession of explosions shook the building. I felt my brain shift inside its skull. They kept coming. Two or three simultaneously. So many I could not count. Then the door crashed open again, and again without thinking I jumped, then slammed my body against it, dropping my IBA.

The barrage of man-seeking bullets began again. I was living a nightmare. Then the AK-47 disappeared a second time and one last explosion shook the building almost off the ground. The door fell to pieces around me. The blast hit me like a bat, knocking me to the floor. I tried to stand, but had fallen on another soldier who was lying face down and under the cot from shoulders up. I shook his leg and called his name. I put my right hand under the cot to check the pulse in his neck. What I felt I will never get out of my head in all my life. I stuck my fingers into what felt like a pool of glue that had been setting for a few hours. My fingers broke through the top layer and into the softness below. Then I found his pulse and my heart sank. I looked at my blood-covered hand in horror.

I was also bleeding in a steady trickle from my neck. I picked up my weapon and ran down the short hallway, which seemed like a mile. I am going to die, I thought.

Then the medic was smacking me awake. I had been hit in the face by debris from the explosion and passed out from blood loss. The medic started an IV, and we waited for the medevac helicopter. I helped carry my soldier in a black body bag to the helicopter. He lay at my feet on the way to the hospital in Baghdad. I said a prayer. My soldier, for whom I had been responsible, my friend, a man who was like a member of my own family, was dead. I broke down and cried.

We reached the emergency room. My leg felt as if someone had poured molten lava along the bones. I was not only bleeding from several wounds to my face, but also the left side of my body was littered with nine shrapnel wounds. The one on my leg was the worst. A nurse poured sterilized water into the hole, which was about four inches long and quite deep, to clean it. The doctor then extracted a jagged piece of grenade—the cause of my excruciating pain.

As I was waiting for church service to begin the next morning in the hospital chapel, my battalion commander, Lieutenant Colonel Bell, and Command Sergeant Major Delgado came to see me and the other wounded soldier. After I explained what had happened, the Sergeant Major asked where the two other soldiers had been at the time. He said that a total of four soldiers had been abducted

Sergeant First Class Billy Wallace receives the Bronze Star with V for Valor, the Purple Heart, and the Army Commendation Medal (ARCOM), September 2007. (Courtesy of Stefanie Wallace)

and mutilated and then killed 25 miles outside of Karbala. My legs went weak and my knees collapsed under me. Delgado hugged me as I again broke down. One of the four soldiers had also been mine. The worst thing that can ever happen is to lose a soldier.

For years to come, January 20th will be a day that haunts me. That night I lost two of my soldiers and I had lived.

For many months I hated those people we called haji. I hated them more than anyone could hate. My unit leadership kept me inside the FOB (forward operating base) and would no longer allow me to go on patrols. They knew I had a personal mission. I would kill every haji I could find. So what if they were not enemy combatants? I would get even. So what if it landed me in prison for the rest of my life? Then one day a thought hit me like a city bus hitting a pedestrian who is not paying attention. We do the same thing to the enemy. We assault and kill them. I have taken the lives of enemy soldiers with the artillery guns I shoot and command. I have seen the photographs of the destruction. I have made a family mourn over losing a child, brother, or husband in this so-called war. I asked myself, Are we better than they? No, we are not. We are one and the same but separated by different belief systems. This realization allowed me to stop hating. The heaviness in my heart lifted.

Sergeant First Class Billy Wallace, US Army, served two tours in Afghanistan and one each in Kosovo and Iraq.
MOS: 13 Field Artillery
HOMETOWN: Cameron, North Carolina

I currently serve as Rear Detachment NCOIC for 2nd Battalion, 321st Airborne Field Artillery Regiment, 4th Brigade Combat Team, 82nd Airborne Division in Fort Bragg, North Carolina. Because of the injuries I sustained in Iraq, I have had multiple surgeries and thus can no longer deploy to combat zones. I have been making preparations for the future in the event I am medically discharged from the Army. Another soldier and I opened a mobile oil change company and motorcycle shop. I also try to spend at least one day a week on the golf course, which gives me time away from the rigors of life and helps me to relax.

HOW EVERY SOLDIER LEAVES Excitement boiled in my stomach as I finished the last of my packing. Pushing and kneading my ACUs and personal hygiene items into my duffle bag left me with beads of salty sweat on my brow. I dipped my combination lock around the eyelet of my duffle with a second sigh. I peeled open the Velcro that kept the pocket on my uniform sealed to make sure I had my ID card. I felt around my neck for the tiny steel beads from which my dog tags dangled. I checked the room for the last time. I had left nothing on the counter but my keys. I imagined that the phone would ring and the person on the other end of the receiver would announce that my flight had been canceled. I would drop my packed green duffle bag with a thump and run around my apartment leaping for joy like Charlie Chaplin, with both legs swinging, one side to the other, as I leapt and clicked my heels together.

The problem was not leaving home, but going to yet another country that has been at war for decades. This time it was Afghanistan. Twice I had already been to Iraq, where people I knew, hung out with, and admired were killed. I looked down at the black metallic bracelets that I wore on both wrists and thought about all five of my friends who had perished over in the big sandbox: Staff Sergeant Seale, Sergeant Mennemeyer, Sergeant Clark, Corporal Zamora, and Corporal Ellis. They too had packed up their belongings and traveled to war, but they hadn't come back. I shook my head. I should be thinking about going to aid in the liberation of the Afghani people. I should be calling my family and friends, saying good-bye and telling them I would be okay, even if I wasn't so sure.

The sound the front door made as it clapped shut signified the end of "civilianhood" and the beginning of 100 percent "soldierhood." I backed the car out of my parking spot and headed to the main intersection, 41A, on my way to the Personnel Terminal hangar at Fort Campbell, Kentucky. I swung the heater knob on the dashboard clockwise to calm the shivers that had less to do with December and more with nerves. The streets seemed overly gloomy too; the wind blew leaves and scraps of paper every which direction.

Once in the terminal I walked smack dab into my platoon sergeant. He directed me to retrieve my weapon from the armory and then return to his location. As I turned I felt a vibration on the lower portion of my right leg. Nerves again? No, this time it was my phone.

"Where are you?" said the voice.

"I'm getting my weapon at the PAX terminal," I said. "I'm here in the center near the rows of chairs." I couldn't believe my ears. This was my third deployment. I had gotten used to being sent off by the unit's Family Readiness Liaison because I have no family nearby. I felt a little special knowing that someone cared enough to show up for my departure to hostile territory.

We sat side by side in two orange plastic chairs in the middle of the terminal.

"I'm going to miss you," he said. "When will you be back on leave?"

I said I didn't know, that I planned to go to Australia for leave. His heart seemed to sink a little. "So, next December, then?"

"Sure," I replied.

Then came the crackling voice of the loudspeaker: "Formation will be in five minutes. Say your final good-byes to loved ones."

Final good-byes, I thought. Families are already panicky about their soldier's well-being, and hearing the word *final* had to scare many of them. The noise in the terminal resonated with "I love you, baby," "Come back to me," "Stay out of harm's way," and "Call me when you land." Children hugged their fathers or mothers as if squeezing them into their bodies. Soldiers used their thumbs to wipe tears from their wives' or husbands' faces.

I turned to my friend, who engulfed me in his embrace. I would not lose control, I told myself. "I'll e-mail you. Don't worry," I said. But this man knew that sometimes you should worry, because he was in the military, too. "There is a 99 percent chance I will be just fine," I said. I smiled, then he smiled, and I turned to head toward the main body formation.

"Brigade, attention!" shouted our chalk leader, signifying the end of the emotional chatter. "Parade rest." He did an about-face to the cluster of family and friends awaiting our departure. Then the brigade commander strutted his way to the podium to give the traditional bon voyage.

"Family and friends of the 159th Combat Aviation Brigade . . ." His voice faded from my attention. Had I turned off the lights in my apartment? How long will we sit in the Personnel Passenger Center? Will the plane crash over the Atlantic? Crash. I had almost forgotten how much flying shakes my soul. I took a swallow of saliva, which felt like fiber powder.

"Good luck on this, your next rendezvous with destiny." The motto of my military post was that each deployment is another rendezvous with history to be remembered by generations and generations to come. Then the lot of us, two hundred soldiers, conducted a unison right-face. As we marched out, banners flashed and cheers echoed our departure from civilization.

The bus ride to the Personnel Passenger Center took only a few minutes, but seemed to take hours. We sat in near silence. My legs lost their feeling and my arms weren't far behind in the numbing process. We were crammed together like flakes of canned tuna in hot sauce. I was carrying my large black personnel assault pack, which weighed about 50 pounds, my weapon, my body armor, and my combat helmet. As the bus swung into the Personnel Passenger Center, soldiers were already rustling to get a head start on their departure from the bus, which hissed as it stopped.

We dropped off our bags at Bay B, and then were instructed to line up to receive our malaria-prevention pills. After a trip to the dining facility for a hot dog and fries, I leaned on the wall of glass that looked out to the Fort Campbell flight line. I couldn't remember it having snowed all winter. To see Kentucky covered by a blanket of snow would have somehow made me feel secure. I stood up and strolled toward a group of soldiers from my company. I stumbled over the bags in my way and plopped down next to one of my acquaintances. We talked about God knows what. Most of the soldiers were spread out on the floor with their heads propped on their assault packs.

About two hours passed and no boarding call. "Hurry up and wait" should be the Army's motto. Soon the refueling was done and the plane was ready for us. The Center exploded with noise as soldiers grabbed their gear and began talking about getting to Afghanistan to kill whoever might be in their way.

I took a seat next to the window. For some reason I always feel more secure knowing I can see if the plane is going down. When I looked out the window as the plane taxied onto the runway, I saw something that made me feel just that much safer—specks of snow. I smiled at my luck. Just then I remembered I hadn't turned off my phone. I reached down, grabbed the phone, and saw I had received a message. I smiled when I read, "See you in Australia. With you, Mike." I sent back a simple reply of "K."

Sergeant Catherine Lorfils, US Army, served in Iraq and Afghanistan.
MOS: 25U Signal Support Systems
HOMETOWN: Miami, Florida

As a Staff Sergeant working at Fort Gordon, Georgia, I teach young impressionable minds about their jobs in the military. My main focus is the Maneuver Control System (MCS). I enjoy both running and scuba diving. One fact I am proud of is that I speak five languages: English, Haitian, Creole, Spanish, French—and Spanglish! My favorite quote: "Life is not measured by the number of breaths we take, but the moments that take our breath away" (anonymous Canadian writer for Carlton greeting cards).

THEY WERE JUST KIDS   A few days after it happens I pick up my cell phone and call my friend Trish in New Jersey. Voice mail. My head drops. I try my sister Lori. She picks up but starts rattling off her own boyfriend problems. Twenty minutes later I decide I've had enough and make an excuse to hang up. I try Trish again. I want to throw the phone into the wall. I give in and fold myself under the covers.

My eyes shoot open. I'm in a sweat. A bad dream. No faces. No screaming. Just the barrel of an AK-47 on my forehead held by a man whose face is completely wrapped with a black-and-white-checkered scarf except for the slit exposing his menacing eyes. I've had enough. If I can't talk to my friend on the phone, I'll write an e-mail.

Dear Trish,

Remember the last time I was on a mission? It was like the end of June, beginning of July, sometime around then. That's when I wrote you last. I was trying to get a flight back to Bagram so I could take my English midterm. Well, the Chinook that was supposed to take me and the Tang had some mechanical problem and was grounded. I talked to the pilot. "I need to get back now," I said. "I'm not staying here another night." Well, whatever it was (maybe I flirted a little), I got us on the one flight that was going out that day. It would not be going to Bagram but to a camp along the way to drop off some supplies. "Why don't you hop on a convoy and meet the flight to Bagram?" the pilot suggested. "Then you'll be good to go."

I was down south at an infantry base where the insurgency and Taliban are fighting hard. The rules of engagement in Afghanistan are generally stricter than they were in Iraq, because basically we're here to win the hearts and minds of the locals rather than to make them angry. But we did what we had to survive.

Well, we start convoying over bumpy dirt roads when, about thirty to forty minutes into the convoy, two kids shoot in front of us. They're a distance away, maybe 50 yards, but all of a sudden they're in the middle of the road, two barefoot boys. The wind ripples their loose cotton shirts and trousers so they look like human flags. They keep standing in the road and waving their arms.

I curse them to fucking move. Fucking bastards. Move! I know that if they don't move we'll run over them in our Humvee. They don't move, and we don't stop. We keep rolling at the same pace. Closer and closer. They keep jumping up and down waving their arms and laughing, yelling something in Pashto. The driver and I look at each other.

"Are you ready?" he says. I don't respond. I look down and load my weapon because I know that kids on the road for no damn reason means the fucking Taliban are out there waiting, hoping we slow down. But we neither slow down nor stop. We roll through. Not even a glance back.

Lately, when I close my eyes I see their faces. The fear when they realize we are not stopping. The mother screaming, a shrieking I can't get out of my head.

When I get back to Bagram, I run into Tracy the next day. She knows something happened on the mission. I don't elaborate, but she starts talking: "I learned from my first deployment to stop caring. Remember how I was when I got back in October? I couldn't sleep for shit. Remember I was up all night bugging you? Shit happens. Put all your little human feelings into a box and seal it shut and never look inside."

But I still feel like I'm alone here. Those kids. They were just kids. That's all I can think about. We just kept rolling, left that screaming mother to pick up the pieces. And that feeling of the tires running over their bodies. I still feel it.

Every time I'm asked how I'm doing, I say fine or that I'm okay. I figure if I say it enough I will be okay. But really, I keep thinking, fucking why didn't they move! Why didn't they fucking get out of the damn way! Why the fuck couldn't I just wait to get back another fucking day! Why did I have to leave that night! What fucking difference did it make if I got back that night or the fucking next morning! There was no fucking difference.

I wish I could get it all fucking out of my head.
Signature . . .

I close my computer, lay it on the footlocker next to my bed. Another sleepless night, I curse to myself. I shut my eyes. I see their faces.

I jump up and grab my Army desert boots and M16 as quietly as I can, trying not to wake my roommates. I creep out the door of my 8 x 10–foot room, frustrated, wishing I could sleep like a normal person. I walk down the B-hut hall and outside into the darkened alley between two parallel rows of fifty plywood boxes just like the one I stepped out of. A gush of wind brushes against my face. Wow, it really does get cold here in Afghanistan.

I sit on a nearby bench designated for smokers. A year ago I would have lit up a Camel filter, I laugh to myself. Not anymore. Been smoke-free a year now. I will not let deployment stress cause me to take a step back. I'm not a punk. I can shake this habit. I don't need anybody to talk to. I'm grown.

Private First Class, Anonymous Female, US Army, served in Afghanistan.

MELTDOWN It was a New York rush-hour lunch on Bagram. I sat in my office with four other sergeants conducting my normal duties, attempting to update all the information and documentation required on each of my soldiers. My desk floated like a boat in a sea of standardized forms punctuated by little mounds of paper clips, silver volcanic islands. I was so busy I didn't know what to do next. That's a cliché, fair enough, but you get my drift. Okay, relax, I told myself. Take a deep breath. What I needed was a break, five minutes on the other side of heaven.

I crossed my office threshold into the Afghanistan sun on my way over to BSOPS (base operations). Like always, it seemed a split second before I was rushing back to the office as if chased by a viper. I noticed a soldier standing outside one of the beige stucco buildings left over from the Soviet occupation. He seemed lost, standing on the cement step staring at, well, at nothing, really.

"Soldier, you okay"? I asked.

"Roger, Sergeant. I'm okay," he said, without ever making eye contact. Before he even finished the words, I was a block of ice, frozen in my tracks. He was missing his usual identifiers: his US Army tag, IR (infrared reflective) flag, ISAF (International Security Assistance Force) patch, and his PFC (private first class) patch. He still wore his name tape, but that was it. I tried again.

"What's the problem? Talk to me?" I took a step nearer as he raised his M16 and inched from the top to the bottom step, and then gently touched the lips of the barrel to the center of my forehead. His finger rested on the trigger, weapon on semi—ready-to-fire, and his breath raced as if he had run miles to reach this moment.

I began edging backward, but he kept up with me.

"I am not the right person for this situation. Let me get that person for you," I said, which strikes me as rather funny now. I mean, who would be the right person to have an M16 pressed against their forehead? I never took my eyes off him, and in turn his were riveted on mine. Three minutes felt like thirty. I drifted back to my grand-

Sergeant Jarrell Robinson visiting his son, Terrell, in Jarrell's grandmother's backyard in Crowley, Louisiana, while on leave from Afghanistan, 2009. (Courtesy of Tyecia J. Robinson)

mother's backyard. I'm walking across the shining Louisiana grass in May complimenting her on a great dinner. My three-year-old son is heavy in my arms, squirming around, batting his feet against my thigh, ready to play, but I *am* playing. I won't let that kid down for nothing! And all the while I never let go of my reflection in that soldier's eyes.

I imagine it is the same feeling a drowning victim has in fighting his way to the surface of the lake, a burst of undirected energy in every limb grabbing toward a point of light. I twisted out of the weapon's sight, dove for it, for an instant even touched the ground with two fingers to steady myself, and then I stumbled over the chunks of gray rock that cover every surface inside a military camp and caused me to run like a drunk. Silence. No shots rang out.

I ran to the smoking area behind BSOPS to get the soldier's supervisor. His NCOIC (noncommissioned officer in charge) and OIC (officer in charge) ran to assess the situation, which is Army for "find out what the hell is coming down." Then I tried to notify the S2's (battalion intelligence staff officer's) OIC and NCOIC. After I checked her office and around the BSOPS area, I just thought, forget it, I'm calling the major on her cell—which is a tricky thing for a sergeant to do, but I figured it couldn't get more important than this.

The damn phone rang and rang until she finally answered.

"Ma'am, there's a situation you should know about." I described what had happened in the short version, as I could not say too much on the phone line.

"I can't make it back right now!" she screamed into the receiver. "I am in a meeting. I'll be there when I get there, Sergeant!"

I was enraged, which is an understatement. But I had to notify others and get the thought of her out of my head.

I left BSOPS and peered around the edge of the building to see the same terrifying scene with a private playing my part this time around. By then the MPs (military police) had been called and were surrounding the soldier and blocking the streets.

When I finished briefing the senior OIC, my job was pretty much done. I could finally find a quiet spot to run through the events of the past half hour, second-guess my actions and reactions, and regain my composure. What somebody said back in the office is that these things happen in a war zone. Everybody's under a lot of stress and everything.

Sergeant Jarrell Robinson, US Army, served in Afghanistan.
MOS: 12Y38, Geospatial Engineer
HOMETOWN: Crowley, Louisiana

I am currently stationed in Fort Leonard Wood, Missouri, as an instructor/writer for the military. As such, I travel around the country to both test and train soldiers on government equipment. I also have a baby on the way. My wife and I hope to learn the sex very, very soon! I am also still attending college, as I would like to become an officer so I can provide the good things in life for my family. My wife is great, and she is rooting for me!

SAT PHONE BLACK OP   My skin, the color of three months' worth of sand, wind, and sweat, longs to feel her touch. I cringe at the idea of my wife imagining me in this state. I have rotated a single change of clothes over the course of four months of dismounted foot patrol in full gear while carrying my weapon in 135-degree heat, and all with no shower. The above equates to a state of stench that can no longer be fathomed even by its owner. Even still, I think she would be glad to see me.

Talking on the phone is a thing of the past in this hellhole. I now occupy a world of communication etiquette, hand gestures, and butchered Arabic. The most substantial conversation I have had over the past few months was about a nasty case of the herp my dismount has. I must stop thinking about my wife. But how in the hell can I lead these men aimlessly about the desert in search of a fight if I do not have a handle on my own psyche? Maybe I should just call her. Yeah, that is the greatest idea ever, except for the fact that it is two in the fucking morning and every piece of brass here is old as shit and falls asleep with the satellite phone in the COC (chain of command) tent anyway.

Wait a minute. They're asleep! "Pssst, hey, dismount. Yeah, you with the herpes and poor judgment. Get your thermals and NVGs (night-vision goggles) with a skull mount and follow me."

"Corporal Moore, are we going to stare at the COC tent with thermals?"

"Now! I need you to focus. Tell me how many people are in there."

"Three, I think. But it is kind of hard to tell."

I wonder if I made the right decision. Inviting the dismount is beginning to look like a bad idea.

"All right," I say, "when I unplug the generator extension cord, the lights will immediately go out. I will then flick my lighter. As soon as I do, I need you to quietly open the side flap of the tent, and then come back behind this berm and hide."

"Are we going to get into trouble?"

"Okay, dude, the idea behind this is to 'borrow' a sat phone so you can talk with your favorite lady of the evening in the States, and I can call my wife. Therefore, it is very important that you are as focused as possible on this objective. Now, do you or do you not want to call your favorite lady?"

"Can I call first?"

"Goddammit! I give you peckers an inch and you automatically take a mile, but yes, you get the first ten."

"You're too good to me, Corporal Moore."

"Shut the fuck up and wait for my signal."

The path to the generator is lit by the green glowing ambience of my NVGs, and the sand beneath my feet softly craters under my weight. "Just like a night raid," I whisper, "soft, smooth, and quiet." As I sit crouched behind the generator, I begin to question whether I have enough ambient light from the moon to show me the way to my rectangular salvation. The increasing heat from the generator soaking through my sweat-stained frog gear is enough to put me over the edge, and I rip the light cord from the generator and flick my Bic in one fluid motion. I watch as my dismount stealthily glides across the sand like a sidewinder and eases the tent flap up to its Velcro homestead.

I look on as the rookie on watch stumbles out of the front hatch of the tent. He is inexperienced in the protocol of a power outage, so he investigates blindly rather than by using the flashlight on his flack. One deep breath and I slip out from behind the generator and glide easily into the night. The tent is darker than I expected, and I know that even though he is a new guy, the watch will check the generator.

Suddenly, I see them. All three satellite phones rest on the charger, with little lime-green lights blinking away like Morse code from God himself. I sidestep the first sergeant and the captain to ease one phone off its charger. A quick glance around the inside of the tent tells me all is well, and the rookie watch dragging his feet in the sand is my cue to exit.

I no longer feel the heat, nor do I care about the occasional whiff of three-month sweat and ass as we make our way back to the truck.

"You're a hell of a dismount, dismount." Back in the safety of the truck, I toss him the phone as his eyes light up in silent awe. "I have no idea how long the battery will last, so seriously, ten mikes and say your good-byes."

"Yes, Corporal!"

"Go make your mother the happiest woman in all of bum-fuck nowhere." His smile is accepting of my banter as he crawls up into the gunner's turret.

I stare into the nothingness that is our home and think about the ill effects of my selfish actions. How will I get the phone back into the tent? However, all repercussions diminish as my new favorite dismount hands me the bulky sat phone. This hunk of junk with an '80s antenna is about to reconnect me with sanity, even if my actions in obtaining it were fucking crazy to begin with. Am I really slipping out here? One ring . . . Okay, no one picks up the phone on the first ring. Two rings . . . Maybe her phone is in her purse. Three rings . . . Pick up the fucking phone!

"Hello?"

Oh, thank you, God. "Hey."

Sergeant Sean Moore, US Marine, served in Iraq.
MOS: 0351 Infantry Assaultman
HOMETOWN: San Marcos, Texas

Since leaving the Marine Corps in 2009, I have been living in San Marcos, Texas, with my wife and taking classes for my dual major, physics and engineering, at San Marcos State University. I am currently a Veterans Advisory Intern for Hays County and the City of San Marcos. In other words, I do stuff to help fellow veterans.

ONE HELL OF A LONG DAY Fifth Battalion, 20th Infantry Regiment, was out on a mission to patrol the streets of Baquba to establish a presence in the neighborhood. It might have been Tahrir or Buritz. I can't remember anymore. The days were running together in my mind even before they were over. Now it's all a violent blur that permeates my daily life.

Baquba is a decimated city about 30 miles northeast of Baghdad on the Diyala River, just outside Iraq's so-called Sunni Triangle. The site has been inhabited continuously since ancient times as a center for agriculture and commerce. The name means "Jacob's House" in ancient Aramaic, and it has been known throughout history to have excellent fruit groves. In fact, the area is still the biggest orange-producing region in the country and currently the capital of Diyala Province. Baquba had been a great city in its prime. When I was there, it was the declared headquarters of the Islamic State of Iraq, a ghost town of pockmarked bricks and broken windows; hence the need for us to conduct daily missions.

The day begins at o-dark-30 with the standard preparations, checks, and briefings. Subordinates are looked over by their leaders, and noncommissioned officers check each other. Everyone is inspected for extra batteries, ammunition, equipment, some food, and lots of water. You never know how long you could be out. We make our way to the objective—out through the gates, lock and load weapon systems, and head down the decrepit main supply route into the downtown area—only to wait an eternity for EOD (explosive ordnance disposal) to arrive and blow an IED (improvised explosive device) with a robot. The EOD guys are almost done setting their explosive charge, so we position our Stryker vehicles in a cleared area. Everyone stays inside the vehicles to prevent unintentional casualties from the controlled detonation of the recently found roadside bomb. Meanwhile, we burn daylight and cigarettes.

Soon we hear a teeth-rattling roar, and the sky goes black with debris. The explosion is big enough to shake the dust off of everything. We laugh nervously, curse, cough, and joke about how close it had felt. Now we can finally get on with our day.

Someone yells out on the radio, "Your truck is on fire!" We look around for the raging inferno, and my squad leader answers, "This is Blue 2. We're fine." Just then, the back door vibrates with frantic knocking. Bam bambam! Someone pops out of one of the back hatches, checks out the scenery, and drops the ramp. Beaver (sans helmet) is screaming at us, "Get the fuck out of there! Now!" A shower of 7.62mm tracer rounds burns through the air.

Then we notice it isn't the EOD team that has triggered the bomb. Weapons Squad's truck is crawling like an anthill freshly kicked. Harris is caught on top of the truck in the camouflage net, screaming. Hilliard and Mathison also huddle on top, screaming over the RPG (rocket-propelled grenade) roars, calling out distance, direction, and description while blasting through their bullets at about 600 rounds per minute. Hilliard cuts the M240B machine gun out of the camo net with his knife when he can't locate his own weapon. And later, after the guy from CASEVAC (casualty evacuation) realizes the M240 had been recovered by 1st Platoon, Hilliard runs to their position. He planned on retrieving the weapon, but he collapses from his injured leg and is taken to the FOB. Matty fires all two thousand .50-caliber rounds during the firefight. He keeps on reloading until the brass casings cover the top of the Stryker and flow down to the floor of the troop compartment.

Beaver crawls into the relative safety of our vehicle, with what we would later learn was a compressed spine, while Helms runs straight in without any visible physical injuries. He never goes out with us again. Cebreros, who had lost his helmet, is dripping blood from his mouth while dragging a shrieking, shrapnel-filled Kindell past me up the ramp of our vehicle. Kindell's femurs are shattered and protruding from his thighs, and the wooden buttstock of his M14 rifle has exploded into body-jamming splinters now lodged in his torso. I can't tell wood from bone.

About this time Cebreros returns to his vehicle to dislodge and remove Private Okada from Weapons Squad's truck under heavy fire, for which he earns the Silver Star. Soon, Harris is strapped to a stretcher on top of the truck, and Tippler, the guy from Human Intelligence, and someone else I can't remember attempt to slowly lower the wailing man down. One of them slips and falls a couple of feet to the ground. His cry is all I hear over the steady roar of the jihad. Almost all of Weapons Squad is rendered worthless in a fraction of a moment.

Our lieutenant has been outside directing fire and calling for backup via the RTO (radio telephone operator). I run up to the lost child who is our Human Intelligence sergeant and bellow directly into his face, "What the fuck are you standing around for? Pick up security!" He shakes his head and complies. Third Squad's vehicle crawls up to provide cover so we can transfer casualties to 2nd Squad's vehicle. Some of the guys from 2nd Platoon come to our aid. Menough, Jordan, and I unleash volley upon volley of fully automatic M249B fire at anything that moves. RPGs and bullets rip the sky, so we crouch as low as possible behind a Stryker. Duncan drops out of the rear of the vehicle with a shoulder SMAW (shoulder-launched multipurpose assault weapon) and obliterates some sorry sap stooping behind a machine gun in a courtyard down the road. While I keep busy shooting at anything that dares present itself, my PL (platoon leader) shoots off a 203 grenade so close behind my head I think it hit me.

When I turn, Duncan, who is almost a head shorter, is shaking him by his body armor. "If you ever do that shit again I'll fucking kill you!" The PL backs off and decides to man the radio.

We are told to take a house behind us to get high ground. My squad enters and clears the abandoned two-story building, regroups in the courtyard, and then advances to the roof, where we are immediately locked down by sniper fire from a three-story building across the road. The guy up there has the advantage but is stupid enough to only use tracers. Lucky for us, every shot fired shows us a clear view of his position, so we fire back and forth for a while.

Hot crimson bolts keep our heads down until a Bradley suppresses the building across the road long enough for an Apache helicopter to engage the target with Hellfire missiles. Quite a show, I must say.

The reports that we receive later indicate that we have killed eighteen or twenty men, but there were most likely more. And while we might have destroyed one group, there will always be others. After all, we're in their backyard. They thought out and ex-

Specialist Karl Mulling and wife, Marie Mulling, in 2010, following the dedication ceremony for a granite memorial erected at the Travis County Courthouse in honor of service members killed since September 11, 2001. The memorial also honors fallen police officers of Austin, Texas. (Courtesy of Connie Gray)

ecuted their ambush well, but we have better equipment and training. I think we were lucky.

The technical term for the device that began the fight is a deep-buried IED. The effect was monstrous. Three-Four Victor wasn't even on top of the kill zone when it blew, and the IED still lifted the rear of their 21-ton Stryker into the air and set the fuel tanks on fire. The electronic systems were fried, the ramp had been nearly ripped from its hinges, the sandbag- and water-bottle-filled seats in the troop compartment were destroyed, and the actual body of the vehicle was warped. It took what seemed all day for the mechanics to haul off the truck. I guess a full-on battle can be worse than your average traffic jam.

After the battle Loveland looked at his watch and declared that it had been just over two hours since the initial attack. We yearned for a trip back to the FOB to regroup and rest. I was as exhausted as if I had just run a marathon and was low on water and ammo.

We were desperate for information about our wounded comrades and asked higher-ups via the radio for a report. They replied that our friends were in surgery or recovering, and that we were to redistribute firepower in our platoon and take our own resupply from the trucks, since we would be continuing with the original mission.

We proceeded to conduct presence patrols for twelve more hours, give or take a few. We couldn't show weakness or any form of retreat. The rest of the day we spent dodging the sonic cracks of bullets and drinking hot, sweet chai served to us in living rooms by Iraqi children and old women until it was dark enough to necessitate mounting NVGs. It had been a long day, maybe the longest. It was the last day that Harris and Okada would walk on their own two feet.

My company had already lost one man since we arrived in Baquba. Brian Chevalier and several others had been injured. Jessie Williams lived and fought alongside us for a few weeks more before he died. Until then he slept in the bunk next to mine at FOB Warhorse when we weren't outside the wire.

Attack Company was hit the hardest overall. Not only had they been ambushed in the palm groves, but they lost a whole vehicle to some old Soviet antitank mines stacked together under the pavement and gained seven KIAs (killed in action), including a Russian reporter who was tagging along with Iraqi soldiers. Why do journalists do that? To venture forth into the fog of battle believing that the pen is mightier than the sword is foolish. Give me a good weapon and plenty of ammunition. I can write about it later.

Specialist Karl Mulling, US Army, served in Iraq.
MOS: 118 Infantry
HOMETOWN: Austin, Texas

I live in Cedar Park, Texas, with my wife and two children. I've been using my GI Bill to take classes for the past couple years but decided that traditional academia is not for me. I do, however, plan to take as many art courses as possible. Most of my drawings and paintings include images of soldiers and battle. Some of my pieces will be shown for the first time at a 2012 Memorial Day festival. I hope that through my work civilians will learn more about the horrors of war and especially about the fighters they take for granted.

On his return home Specialist Karl Mulling was diagnosed with both PTSD (Post-Traumatic Stress Disorder) and TBI (traumatic brain injury). The two pieces that follow are written by Marie Mulling, Karl's wife. In them she describes the difficulties she, her husband, and her children face in their day-to-day life following his deployment.

MARIE MULLING

PROTECTION   I spent a rare night away from my husband and children, house-sitting for my mother, watching John Hughes flicks on VHS from Goodwill for fifty cents. I returned home refreshed on Saturday morning, happy to see my family. I wandered through the house and met them in the backyard, mowed where the Little Tykes plastic slide and swing reside but left mostly wild. The kiddie pool was full, ten inches of water. My children seemed content, their wet swimsuits lounging in the tub, their dry clothes on. They had missed me but were happy to have spent the day with Daddy, who is more lax about things like making them pick up after themselves.

Across our yard, I saw the rusty lawn mower. I asked our daughter if Daddy had stayed with them while they were in the pool. I was hoping he had shown the presence of mind not to mow while they were sitting in water up to their chins. Worse, my daughter told me, he had gone inside the house to pee. My redheaded two-year-old and my elfin five-year-old cannot swim.

Now if I leave town for the weekend and my husband is home with our children, he is not allowed to bathe them. No more swimming. Nor is he allowed to cook, because he forgets the chicken nuggets in the oven. He calls me from two streets away, lost. He cannot orient himself. The streets have changed their names. They have made a maze of themselves. He is lost. Can I tell him where he is?

These are the bad days. A good day was when the psychiatrist at the VA confirmed what we already knew, that he has brain damage. He processes slowly. He has short-term memory loss, probably from driving over an IED. He called me the next day from Iraq and made light of it, this incident that would shape our lives. This TBI. He had two black eyes and wasn't allowed to sleep. I was awakened at 5 a.m. when he called from Iraq. I did not care he had driven over a bomb. I was happy to get a phone call from him, not someone else with worse news from an equally unknown number. I didn't know what TBI meant yet. I was not thinking about PTSD. I was still trying, like him, to survive the deployment.

Now we are trying to survive the redeployment. Now he looks for snipers on roofs and checks our perimeters. He is anxious driving under overpasses or by bloated roadkill. He is waiting for another explosion. He does not see our toddler wandering away in the mall because he is making sure we have a safe exit strategy and a good defense should someone in Macy's open fire on us. He cannot bathe our children because it does not occur to him that something as innocuous as water could hurt them. But he will protect them from snipers and roadside bombs.

OUR LIVES TODAY I recently spent a weekend with the mothers of the girls in my daughter's Girl Scout Daisy troop. One of the mothers mentioned her maid, and I laughingly stated that our family is closer to her maid's income bracket than her own, since our income is $35,000 a year. Another mom wondered about the poverty level for a family of four, unintentionally implying that we must be living below it. In fact, we have finally made it above the poverty line! Karl can no longer work due to short-term memory loss, and I am unable to work because I am the caretaker for both of our children as well as for Karl.

The process of receiving compensation for Karl's injuries took a great deal of persistence. We first filed for disability through the VA. Next, Karl was sent to doctors for C&P exams (Compensation and Pension). Then we waited. Eventually, we received a judgment. Our next step was to file an appeal with a DAV (Disabled American Veterans) office. Then, again, Karl was examined by a number of doctors. We waited. And so it went until after three years of appeals, Karl has finally been granted an 80 percent disability rating.

Karl finally received compensation in part because I kept a "memory journal." For one month I documented each and every of his memory lapses. Although Karl's payment is only $1,700 a month for our family of four, I was also granted a caregiver's stipend through VeteransPlus. I have also been granted health insurance, which brings us to a livable wage. We will continue to appeal until

Karl receives a 100 percent rating. When a young soldier sacrifices the rest of his or her working life to ensure the freedom of a country, that country should stand tall the way Karl did, and salute him!

Marie Mulling is the wife of Specialist Karl Mulling, whose piece appears above, on page 23.

COINCIDENCE I don't remember the day, month, time, or even his name. It was about halfway through my deployment to Iraq. I had just been switched to night shift in the DFAC (dining facility) when I got the call. I was needed because of President Bush's surge. I had heard stories from other girls. Some passed out, others vomited, but most cried and just refused to do the job. I had said no to being placed among their ranks once already. It wasn't mandatory or anything. Just a new skill and a new experience. I didn't understand the big deal. I felt excited and a little nervous the first time. They said the smell would be horrible. But overall I thought I was ready and I was. Being ready isn't what I needed to worry about. It's how to deal with the events afterward.

He is white, maybe twenty, medium height, gray eyes the color of a rainy sky. His BDUs (Battle Dress Uniform) look like they've been rolled in dirt. And the body odor. Well, it's bad. But who wouldn't be dirty and wrinkled after such a long flight in a C-130, and Baghdad isn't even his last stop.

A few days earlier he had come through the line in the DFAC. I was serving lasagna. It was a Friday night. I looked up through the cloud of food steam and kidded around with him a little bit, just for fun. He said he was leaving that night for a FOB. Then he smiled, said thanks when I spooned a pile of dinner onto his plate, and kept moving.

Now, the second time I see him, he lies on this table, a big chunk of his left leg missing and a flimsy piece of bloody meat holding his calf and thigh together. The explosion burned all the hair and skin off his skull, which is the whitest white I have ever seen. The room has a metallic smell so strong I can taste it. I keep looking into his left eye. The right was burned along with the right side of his face. It feels like he is looking at me, too, the moment he realized he was not going to make it frozen in a flat, gray stare. Regret at life ending so soon. Somebody in the room said his Humvee was rocketed. He is heavy.

I shift his body by putting one arm under his waist and the other over his stomach and under the hip on his right side. I remove his keys and Gerber. That's it. I drop it all in a small cardboard box with the soldier's name already written in Marks-a-Lot across the top.

We bag, tag, and put him in a casket. Then the flag is carefully draped over the rounded top. We carry him to the freezer. I wash up, change from scrubs into my uniform, and drive back to the DFAC. It is dark out, the kind of black that makes me want to curl up with a sheet over my head and a flashlight. I am thinking of all the things that should happen: loss of appetite, nightmares, anxiety, the usual female stuff. As soon as I hit the DFAC, I eat because I had missed dinner. I have pollock, which is dry, steamed rice, and bread hot from the oven, which I spread thick with butter. I eat like I have never seen food before. My friends and I laugh, joke around, and watch movies until time to serve the next meal. I am so proud of myself. I haven't cried, passed out, or vomited like the other girls. I have made it through the night!

For the rest of the deployment I stop harassing the soldiers who come through the DFAC. In fact, I don't really see them anymore. They don't exist. I go to the morgue when called in, and when I shut the door behind me, I forget everything.

When we closed the casket, it was supposed to have been the last time I would see him. I had never watched the news before my deployment, and when I got back to the States I avoided CNN like a doe running for her life when she spots a predator. After I had been home a few months, I met another soldier, his eyes gray like the one on that morgue table. I tried to avoid him, but he was a good friend of a friend, which made it impossible. That's when it started. That one gray eye looking back at me, the flecks in it clear as if I had last stared into them this morning. Why have I died so young? it would ask.

I felt guilty. I was afraid of who I might be hurting by my depression. I began avoiding my friends, family, and coworkers. The world was closing in on me. I had everything except a raison d'être. I finally made it to the chaplain's office, where I cried like the other girls. I started going to church and little by little became my old self. Life is hard, downright horrible at times, but it's better to be here than to subtract yourself from the equation.

Private Second Class, Anonymous Female, US Army, served in Afghanistan.

B-HUT BLUES As I lay reading over the latest copy of *Men's Health* magazine, I listen to the 120th day of wind produce its violent music as it pops the tin roof back and forth. The Great Voice, the eerie public-address system that permeates even the gray rock that covers almost every inch of ground here, spits out a familiar monotone phrase, "The aerial gunnery range is now hot."

Do any of us really know what the hell this means? Will someone please enlighten me? What we do know is that in the next few minutes there will be several big booms, friendly fire, maybe practice shots. I glance up from the pages of my magazine to one of the plywood walls of my room and the 3 x 5–foot American flag I've hung there. I well up with pride. Then I look to the other wall lined with pictures of my wife and children, and my love of my country turns to sorrow.

Shake it off, I tell myself. You can't get distracted with thoughts of home, which will send you spiraling in a whirlwind of depression. The greatest obstacle I face is replacing the images of family and home with those of death and war, but I must, or I will go insane. I look back at the plywood walls of my B-hut. The thought crosses my mind that if every soldier, sailor, airman, or marine had written their story on the wall in the past ten years, there might not be room to write my own. Every war veteran has a story to tell. Is society ready to listen?

I return to scanning the "Six Weeks to Six-Pack Abs" article, and then take a quick glance at the University of Maryland calendar on the wall, back to magazine, to calendar, to magazine, as if each time I look another day will have passed. Not a good thing to do, so I drop the magazine on the floor and vow to get some sleep.

What the hell was that? A bottle rocket? No, no bottle rocket! The bed shakes from the percussion of the blast. "AMBER ALERT, AMBER ALERT," the Great Voice bellows. I scan my extremities. Not hit. I roll out of bed, don my battle rattle, including Kevlar helmet, and head for a bunker, which is full of people yelling questions: Is everyone okay? What's going on? Where did it hit? Is everybody accounted for? Someone shouts that a mortar hit a couple of B-huts away. We sit like ducks in a row in a cement bunker on a low cement bench. We sit bent over in the pitch black. The deadening silence is soon interrupted by our friend the Great Voice: "All clear, all clear."

I return to my room and reposition myself in bed, but sleep at this point is impossible. I toss and turn, my mind flooded with thought after thought. What if the mortar had hit my B-hut? Would I have survived or would my wife have been handed a flag? I am just a few weeks from going home, and I would be really pissed off if I died now. If I were going to get killed, I would rather it have been in the first few days than after I endured this entire deployment.

Sergeant First Class Michael Bramlett, US Army, served in Afghanistan and Saudi Arabia.
MOS: Confidential
HOMETOWN: Clarkesville, Georgia

I am currently still serving in the military with nineteen-plus years. I enjoy spending all the time I can with my wife and three children. I have learned not to take the time I have with family for granted. I want to thank all military members, past and present, for their service and sacrifice to our country.

BOMBED   I sit in the back of a van bumping along a dirt road that circles the perimeter of Bagram Air Base. The road, just inside the concertina wire, opens to views of Afghan villages, small mud huts melting with age, home sweet home to the young children herding goats, stopping only to stare with dark eyes as we pass. I zone out to my graduation from Bolton High less than three years ago. I knew nothing about either the military or terrorism. Every plane looked the same, and all bombs did the same thing, went BOOM. Now here I am, just weeks from my twenty-first birthday, about to enter a building where I am expected to be the expert on which bombs to drop and where. My entire body shakes as F-15s take off directly behind me. The roar echoes in my head.

I had arrived the evening before on a two-hour flight in a cramped C-17 from Manas Air Base in Kyrgyzstan. All nerves and anxiety, I walked across the runway, my 110-pound frame weighed down by 40 pounds of body armor. The runway lights lit the cold January night, revealing the slight outlines of mountains completely surrounding us. I took a deep breath to control my overwhelming mix of emotions and choked on blowing dust and jet fuel.

In the morning light I walk tentatively down the hall to a wooden door still painted with the tiger-striped mascot of the previous squadron. On my way to the back room and my desk, I pass a metallic gray Styrofoam human skull dangling from the ceiling over a cluster of six or so desks. Army humor. Below the skull a small sign reads, "Army Ground Liaison Officers." We would be working hand in hand. I am an intelligence analyst. It is my job to keep the fighter pilots and weapons systems officers flying the F-15 Strike Eagles safe. Keep them safe so they can keep the soldiers on the ground safe. Eight missions per day.

For the next few months I would follow the same routine. I check the dry-erase board behind me. At the top in bold black letters it reads, "Troops in Contact," better known as TIC. This morning the board is still empty. That's a good sign. No one getting shot at, at least not yet. I sit in my wobbly rolling chair and wipe the dust from my computer screen, and then type in my classified password. Now logged on, I search for the best information to give my guys prior to today's missions. I worry they will be shot down, yet my tiresome daily warning sounds like a mother's scream after her children as they head off to school.

I read through the list: suicide bomber threats to camps, rockets located, insurgents training to attack Bagram. My eyes pass over the words as if reading a dull article from *Cosmo*. Just then four members of the two-ship enter the room for their mission brief. I walk across the floor, take my place in front of the large TV screen in front of a row of plush leather chairs, and begin to speak. Standing center stage I become the weather girl and mission specialist I was trained to be.

A small group of people enter the room, wrinkled and exhausted, but excited. One sets down a blackened green helmet bag, quietly takes out a few folded sheets of paper, and stands near the large table in the center of the room, waiting for me to finish speaking. I give the expected reminder as to what the pilots should do if shot down. Having completed my briefing, I hand the black slide changer off to a large Army man and walk over toward the pilot in the now-familiar tan flight suit, all the standard patches still removed for the five-hour mission he just completed. Indentations from his oxygen mask still mark the bridge of his nose and run across his cheeks like webs. He looks down into his notes as he tells his story of what happened in the air. Nothing significant. A good sign. Every day is the same, brief and debrief, write reports. I lose track of days.

The sun has just finished its rising over the mountains on a day somewhere in the middle of the week. Spring is coming. The snow has faded away. Already the morning is busier than usual. A few guys sit around waiting to go on missions. A couple hang out watching a movie. In the background the infinite sound of drum-rolling rock music beats on. I glance over the desk only to see the bright red line flash across the screen of black and blue text. The line says what it always says: troops somewhere in Afghanistan taking fire. But today the text continues, "DUDE 21 to support." The foghorn yells as the alert crew scramble to duty, grab their gear and run full speed to the F-15s. Seven minutes from the foghorn's yell to the sound of afterburners filling the air as four jets disappear over the surrounding mountains.

I watch the chat room on the screen, watch the ongoing firefight unravel in words in front of my eyes. Bits of play-by-play description quickly run together. "Enemy fire in the tree line. Request 1x GBU-31 (Guided Bomb Unit) on the target." I know what this means. I would have been over my head years before.

I wait in slow-motion time for the crew to return. When the back door opens against the bright sunlight, I see the dark outlines of our men and women. My handwriting sprawls across the page as they give their detailed report.

The scene plays like a film. Trees line one side of a narrow dirt road. On the opposite side friendly forces slow their convoy due to disturbances in the road. A standard setup. Stop the convoy and then attack. Sure enough, artillery rounds blast the immediate area of our forces. Between returning shots, the joint aerial controller calls for support from above. My crew drops its first bomb of the day. In seconds the insurgents firing from the seemingly safe cover of trees will be blown away by the force of 2,000 pounds of explosives falling on their exact location.

The coordinates from the location of the firefight have passed from the ground to the aircrew thousands of feet above. All that was left was for them to be entered into the bomb's GPS, and it would internally glide itself to the enemy waiting below. Just before the bomb hit, the exploding sound of jet engines must have given the insurgents a warning of the destruction to come.

A few of the bad guys might be smart enough to run and manage to briefly survive. These "squirters," as we call them, run from the trees to a motorcycle lying somewhere slumped along the side of the road. They pop the gas, rushing full speed down the potholed dirt path, thinking they can outrun the jets above. In the sky my aircrew receives approval to reengage. On the black-and-white screen in the backseat of the F-15, the weapons system officer uses the targeting pod to pay close attention to the men. He steadily aims the laser, which is invisible to the natural eye, on the moving target. The 500-pound GBU-12 drops off the wingtip and guides itself along the path of laser that steadily continues to follow the enemy. Tracing the line, the bomb slices through air, landing only feet from the motorcycle's front wheel. Success! The crew passes the news to our forces on the ground, who only minutes before were literally fighting for their lives.

After the debriefing I head back to my corner to begin my reports. I barely settle into my seat when the door opens with the return of another crew. Gathering my papers and my favorite black Sharpie, I walk over to the table to stand across from the three female crew members to begin another debrief. Again, a firefight. This time inside the walls of a small village.

Standard clearing operations meant to weed out insurgents broke into full battle. A building on the outskirts of the village was a known stronghold for insurgents. Those firing at our forces were seen reloading their weapons just outside. Other enemy fighters had scattered inside the village, and our men concealed themselves in collapsed houses, under vehicles, wherever they could. The known stronghold became a necessary target to give our soldiers an opportunity to escape enemy fire.

Radioing from the ground to the flight providing overwatch, the JTAC (joint tactical air controller) passes the necessary 9-line giving all information needed for the airstrike. A GBU-38, 500 pounds of explosives on a GPS, glides to its target thousands of feet below.

With the stronghold destroyed, the resupply of enemy ammo has been decreased, but the firefight continues. Due to the possibility of collateral damage because of the location of the enemy, bombs are no longer an option. Once again passing a 9-line, JTAC requests a new attack. This time with a gun. Lining up the F-15 over the location of enemy forces, the aircrew drops altitude and fires off one hundred rounds of 20mm along the path of their targets. Because of a near miss on the first pass, two jets alternate strafing passes until the firing ceases and the jets run out of rounds.

I once again sit down, now to finish both sets of notes, or to start them, for that matter. Over my shoulder I watch as the crew reviews the weapons videos. The stories I just heard unfold in black-and-white. I can hear the crew talking to the soldiers on the ground while the bullets are impacting all around them. The JTAC sounds like a young man, twenty-something. He's out of breath. I can hear the longer-than-usual pauses between sentences and targeting lines. He's dodging rounds and finding cover.

After the crew's sixth strafe pass, his voice brightens. "The fire's stopped! Thank you! Thank you for all your help!"

I think about how guilty I sometimes feel about sitting behind my safe little desk while there are so many men and women in fire-fights every day, even every hour, in Afghanistan. I know the JTAC wasn't thanking me directly, but I will never forget the sound of his breathless voice. I know that my crews would not be able to safely protect the soldiers in the field without my help. I know at this moment that there is nowhere else I would rather be than helping protect those who are risking their lives to protect me.

Senior Airman Michal Sakautzki, US Air Force, served in Afghanistan.
AFSC: 1NO51 Intelligence Analyst
HOMETOWN: Glenside, Pennsylvania

No longer in the military, I am now living in Orlando, Florida, with my husband and baby girl. I recently completed my bachelor's degree in psychology and will be pursuing a master's in criminology and forensic psychology. I enjoyed traveling the world during my time in the military, especially to such countries as England, France, Germany, Italy, the Czech Republic, the Netherlands, and Spain.

THE HARDEST GOOD-BYE   I see her for the first time in many years. She is not what I remember at all. Her once flowing black hair has thinned. It hangs wispy over the blue and white flowers that cover her hospital gown, adding such age to her face. Her frame is fragile and frail, her eyes sunken, cold spaces. No one has been home for quite some time. A suffocating blanket of guilt wraps tight around me. I abandoned her. I am the reason for her lifeless, vacant body. She is dying. I stand at a distance, going over and over what I will say, hesitant to approach our ailing reality.

She was born Tiffany Tyler and by marriage became Tiffany Prey, but she will always be Auntie Tip to me. We spent breezeless summers in front of cooling fans and ate sliced watermelon that left us with sticky fingers and huge smiles. My mother worked long and underpaid hours for a recycling manufacturer, and my father drove in all the cardinal directions in his semi truck to make a living. My brother and I spent countless memorable hours with Auntie Tip. One life-changing summer Auntie Tip almost burned our apartment down; she had gone to take the overflowing trash out and left the stove on. My brother, Dustin, and I lay on the couch fast asleep. We were only awakened by the fire alarm. It literally saved our lives. Now I clear my throat and swallow my tears. Time to greet Auntie Tip.

"Hi, Auntie," I say. I grab her and hold on so tight that I fear my grip will squeeze the life out of her, and I quickly loosen my arms.

"Tanya, I am missed you like crazy. You go off to the Army, and you never look back for us," says Auntie Tip.

My mind strays for a minute. Her cold hands on my sinking soul bring me back. Even with all that people whisper, I am not afraid to touch and hold her. Auntie Tip has AIDS. She's known for four years, but did not have the heart to tell me. She tries to look me in the eyes, but neither of us can hold our gaze. Our small talk goes on for several minutes, but I can only think about how much longer I will have her in my life.

"When are you due to deploy again?" she asks.

I do not want to answer her. My response will only reveal that I will once again be leaving. "At the end of the year," I say.

It is now July. My husband and I are in Miami for a family reunion. Auntie has been in the hospital several times recently. First it was double pneumonia and a plummeting white-cell count. Then a myriad of problems. Would this be my long good-bye?

Too soon, it is time to leave for the airport, time to return to the life I now lead 886 miles from the city that was once my home. I am leaving Auntie Tip behind. She has five children who she will not see through college or even possibly through the year. Auntie Tip is also hooked on drugs that have claim on her every desire. I am fortunate to have known her when she was younger, without her high.

"Good-bye," I say.

"No, not good-bye. I'll see you later," she says.

I take an exaggerated breath as I realize that this is the hardest good-bye I have ever said.

Sergeant Latayna Orama, US Army, served three tours in Iraq and one in Afghanistan.
MOS: 79S Career Counselor
HOMETOWN: Lehigh, Florida

I recently decided to explore the world! My first flight will take me to Japan in August of this year. I have discovered a love for culture and adventure. Although traveling is quite costly, I believe it to be worth any and all sacrifice. I also just turned twenty-seven in April, time to get serious about furthering my education. I am even considering a technical school, a big change for me. I also hope to start a family in the next few years. I really look forward to that adventure. I have learned that failure only comes when you fall three times and get up only twice.

ROUTINE MISSION 0400 hours. Myself and four others from my scout platoon infiltrate a palm grove under cover of darkness. It's already 80 degrees and the humidity reminds me of back home in Philadelphia during a heat wave in July. This was supposed to be a routine mission. Gather intel on possible river-crossing points used by Al Qaeda insurgents to supply weapons to local militias. "Easy mission," I said when I was briefed. "Just another waste of time."

We've already been in Iraq six months. This is my second deployment here in three years. Three guys in our platoon along with our translator were killed by an IED attack last month, so now we're all looking for a reason to kill somebody. But we never could have predicted what would happen on this "easy" mission.

I'm on point when we come upon a barbed-wire fence lined with thick shoots of bamboo. The fence is tall enough that I can't see what's on the other side. The terrain is rough, and palm trees create a thick canopy over our heads. It rained yesterday, which makes the mud trail slippery as ice, and we're all sliding. I look over my shoulder to the platoon leader. "What do you want to do, Sir?" He motions to breach the wire so we can find out what's beyond the camouflaged perimeter.

Once over the fence we face three trails all headed in different directions. Each trail is lined with the same fencing as was the perimeter. We find ourselves in a maze. Like mice searching for cheese, we choose the middle trail. Fuck it. If something bad is going to happen in here, I'd rather go straight to the bastards and split them in half, I think.

I can no longer hear the traffic from the highway. We have walked about two klicks into the palm grove and away from any backup support. Two thoughts ripple down my spine: I have never experienced such silence, and it would be too easy to get lost in this place.

Then a noise. A bearded man turns the corner ahead on a bike. I'll never forget his expression. He slams on his brakes, drops the

Sergeant Kevin Zimmerman takes a break in Baquba, Diyala Province, Iraq, 2007. Members of the 1-12 Cav, 1st Cavalry Division, had been dropped by Black Hawk helicopter in 120-degree heat to search and clear houses; the village was thought to be protecting Al Qaeda insurgents. (Courtesy of Staff Sergeant James West)

bike in the mud, and takes off running. This isn't good, I think. I turn back to the PL again and shake my head. He agrees but for some reason signals to keep going. "Just wave at whoever you see," he whispers. Hearts and minds, my ass. Next, an old woman opens the door of a mud hut and walks hesitantly out. Her face has that What-the-hell-are-US-soldiers-doing-in-this-place look. She takes off back inside the hut and slams the door behind. Here we go, I think. I reach down to my vest and pull out a 40mm grenade and load it into my launcher, a sound that is followed by the rest of the squad doing the same.

POP! POP! POP! The shooting comes from behind us to the north. I turn. The other four guys in the squad are running toward me. We're stuck in the middle of a goddamned path with no cover. Bullets snap and whiz past my head. My first firefight. I am terrified but would later learn to just get pissed off when it happens. I shoot off a grenade from my launcher. I can't see any of these fuckers! I turn and run with the rest of the guys.

Fifty yards to the south the path splits. Since each path is lined with the same barbed-wire fence as the perimeter, we're sitting ducks. We find cover and stoop in a defensive position, Demuth and Rogers on the left and me on the right. The PL is behind trying to call for backup on the radio. The shots keep popping. I can't see a soul, but the enemy is close enough to smell their body odor. Dirty bastards don't understand hygiene like we do. We literally take turns firing toward the smell. They already know how many of us are here, so no use volleying fire. We try to conserve ammo in case we need it later. That's when the silence returns. Not a fuckin' sound.

"Did we kill 'em?" Rogers asks. Before anybody has time to answer, the shooting starts again. This time from the west. Holy shit! These fuckers have us in an L-shaped ambush, which is a textbook US military move. These guys are well-trained and motivated. The PL tries to call in air support, but the palm grove is so dense we can't get a signal. The rest of the platoon is two or three miles away. Nobody knows we're under attack. It's the five of us on our own. No medic and no radio. If one of us gets wounded or killed, nobody's getting out of here alive. My PL looks at me.

"What the hell do we do now?" I say. "We got to get the fuck out of here!" Adrenaline can make men do crazy shit. The first three guys damn near do flips hopping over the barbed wire so we can move out to the south and get out of the kill zone. Myself and Sergeant Demuth, Meat as we call him, stay behind while the others move back. We both aim our grenade launchers. Luckily, I have a bag full of grenades. Back and forth we go. He shoots high. I shoot low. We fire grenade after grenade, trying to halt the enemy's advance on us. We see a chance to break contact and run south with the rest of the squad. We might have killed none of them or maybe twenty. We would never know.

Our map shows we'll hit a river if we move due south. The Diyala River winds like a snake through the province. Just our luck it loops all the way back around the area where we were ambushed and right back to the police station, which is where we live. Our escape plan is to find the river, stay low, and make it to the platoon alive. Pretty simple. We figure we're about five klicks from our outpost. It's noon, and the temperature has risen to 100 degrees. Not a cloud in the sky. Humidity and mosquitoes make the situation worse. And the mosquitoes in Iraq are so big we've named them the Iraqi Air Force. We're beginning to feel the effects of the heat when the PL calls a water break. Nobody argues. We still hear random shots in the distance. The enemy wants us to shoot back so they can come kill us. Not gonna work.

By this time we're cross loading ammo and water. We're each wearing 75 pounds of gear along with full packs. As we move north along the river, we come upon a clearing and try to radio again.

"Bone X-Ray, Bone X-Ray, this is Stalker 2," I call over the net. Silence. The PL takes the hand mic and tries. Static. That's good. Almost in range. I boost the radio power and finally somebody hears us.

"Thank God," Meat says. Then the shooting starts back up. Five or six men appear across the river. We all return fire while the PL stays on the net with our TOC (tactical operations center).

"Call in some fuckin' mortars, Sir!" I yell between shots. He gives the grid and calls for indirect fire from a mortar team at the outpost occupied by the rest of our platoon. Within seconds mortars rain down on those bastards like a hailstorm from hell. Shrapnel rips through the enemies' bodies like hot knives through butter. Beautiful.

"Stalker 6, this is Bone X-Ray."

"This is Stalker 6. Go ahead," says the PL.

"Find an LZ (landing zone) for helicopter extraction. If you can't find one, a Special Forces platoon in boats along the river to the north is ready to extract you." Find an LZ in this fucking mess? No fuckin' way.

We keep moving north with the river to our left. Our backup plan involves dropping our gear in the river and swimming to the other side. We hope it won't come to that. The terrain is rough along the river, but nobody complains. We each fall at least a half dozen times. I'm still on point when I find a clearing in the palm grove big enough to land a chopper. Soon we hear a loud rumble, and then the high-pitched whine of a jet-engine-powered M1 tank. Across the river three tanks appear and set up defensive positions. One of the hatches opens and a hand sticks out giving us a thumbs-up.

We're good. Right? We found an LZ and have three fuckin' tanks watching our backs. Wrong! Across the LZ on the eastern side of the river the shooting erupts. Are these guys dumb? Shooting at tanks? Actually, they are quite smart. They know the tanks won't fire directly over our heads to get to them. So here we are, defending ourselves once again. What those bastards don't know is that two Apache attack helicopters have just arrived in the sector to find us.

"Any Stalker element, this is Red Wolf 1. Over," we hear over the net.

The PL responds, "Red Wolf 1, this is Stalker 6. We're taking fire from the eastern side of this clearing." The next words that come across the net I will never forget because they made us all laugh right in the middle of a firefight.

"Not for long!" replies Red Wolf 1, the pilot of one of the Apaches. He's right. A few rockets and 30mm chain aimed at their ass stops the shooting real quick.

With so much going on, we don't even realize the Black Hawk helicopter has arrived and is circling to land.

"Pop some smoke," I say. Myself and Meat each throw a smoke grenade on either side of the clearing to hide the Black Hawk's landing and cover our sprint to the chopper. The bird lands. I see the door gunner wildly waving his arm at us to jump on. One by one we take off running. I'm the last on board. The pilot doesn't even wait for us to fasten ourselves in. He does a vertical takeoff straight up. Shit! From the air we see we are a lot farther than we had thought from the police station. We must have gotten turned around in that palm grove and backtracked.

The wind on my face feels like a sigh of relief from God. Soaked in sweat, we don't say a word the entire flight back to FOB Warhorse, where our brigade is stationed. Meat taps me on the shoulder and holds out a Marlboro Red. No words, just a nod and a smile. As we land at Warhorse, I light that sucker up and inhale the sweet tobacco. The battalion commander meets us at the landing pad and welcomes and debriefs us.

We hop into the back of a pickup truck. Lieutenant Colonel Goins sits us down and says, "So, were you guys out there looking for that suspected Al Qaeda training camp?"

What the fuck did he just say? A fucking Al Qaeda training camp?

"No, Sir, we were unaware of any suspected camp, but I think we confirmed it's there," I say. The PL tells us to leave and grab some chow. The other unit that lives on our pad is having a barbeque: ribs, chicken, steak, baked potatoes, and salad. While I'm out doing this shit these poges are having a fucking cookout? They invite us. We decline.

"You guys look pretty rough," they say. "Bad day out there?" Nobody says a word. The four of us grab a sandwich at the chow hall and wait for the next bus to the police station. We're going back out in an hour, we hear, to link up with our platoon. Good, I think. I can't stand to be around these guys and their fucking barbeque. And I'm not the only one who feels this way.

Demuth and I eat, and then sit together on the ground, backs up against some sandbags. After about fifteen minutes of silence and about three cigarettes, he finally speaks. "Another day at the office."

I look up into the sky and laugh. "Just another day."

Sergeant Kevin Zimmerman, US Army, served in Iraq and Afghanistan.
MOS: 19D Calvary Scout
HOMETOWN: Austin, Texas

I live in Austin, Texas, where I attend Austin Community College full-time. I am majoring in kinesiology and hope to become a physical education teacher. My dream is to someday coach hockey. My wife and I are looking forward to starting our family soon.

A WOMAN, A BOXER As a boxer, I have been thrown many blows. Some were harder than others and some even knocked me down. Losing my parents at an early age was the experience that took me to the ring.

Round 1 My mother had been my oxygen. She supported me in every way a mother could. She believed in me and always told me I could accomplish even when I felt I could not. She was my home. Without her I couldn't have stood on my own.

Round 2 I barely remember my father. His absence left a sense of incompletion in me. I've longed for the love of a father and to experience the affection I never received, a father to carry me on his shoulders when I was tired, to rescue me from harm's way, to protect me from others.

Round 3 Losing them was like getting dealt a combo or an upper-cut that left me out of breath. But the more you are hit, the tougher you become. Those rounds have made me a stronger person. They shaped me into a rock.

Round 4 I'm tough, unbreakable, and steadfast. The blows I've taken did not break me. Instead they helped make me. If I hadn't been knocked down, I wouldn't have learned how to stand firm. If I wasn't a boxer who took blows until I was a rock formed by them, I could not have learned to tolerate adversity as a soldier.

Round 5 I'm a warrior, determined, who accepts challenge and strives for excellence. My struggles taught me to endure. As a soldier, I look forward to my future as I press through each mission on the battlefield. It takes courage for a soldier to walk into the unknown. I serve with pride, believing my experiences have brought out the best in me.

Round 6 I'm a winner because I believe. God alone gave me the strength to become a boxer. I can breathe again! I'm standing alone now! God used my experiences as tools to shape me. He told me in 2 Timothy 4:5 to "endure hardship" as a soldier and in Joshua 1:7 to "be strong and courageous." It was God alone who made me who I am.

Private Veneta White, US Air Force, served in Afghanistan.
AFSC: 2R1X1 Maintenance Management Production
HOMETOWN: Andrews, South Carolina

I've recently returned from a vacation in Hong Kong, an amazing experience. In a few weeks I'll be transitioning with the military to March AFB in California, a place I've always wished to live. I plan to complete my bachelor's degree in nursing and to become a traveling nurse. And thanks to the Army I can make that happen! The military has been a blessing, the vehicle for turning dream into reality.

LITTLE GIRL, RUN . . . IT'S NOT SAFE HERE It's 150 degrees and the breeze feels like a hair dryer blowing finely powdered dirt at close range into my eyes, nose, ears, mouth, and even under my clothes. Everyone on the team wears a neck gaiter and pulls it up over his face in order to breathe.

I thought today might be uneventful, but one of the commander's runners walks my direction. "Hey, he wants you to grab your gear and be ready to roll out in an hour."

We all know who "he" is. I am an armorer, and before deploying I helped fix and calibrate multiple weapons systems in our battalion. The commander wants me in his Humvee whenever he goes on a convoy so if he runs across one of his units with an inoperable weapon I can fix it. Or, say we get ambushed and a weapon malfunctions, then he has someone to correct the problem.

After the first few ambushes I began to think of the adrenaline rush as normal, which allows me to focus less on when an attack might happen and more on my part in the countermeasures.

I grab my flak vest, Kevlar helmet, and load of ammunition. On my way to the staging area, I stop by my storage CONEX (military shipping container) and pull out a couple of AT-4s (antitank ordnance) and a box of grenades, and then drop the keys off with my first sergeant in case I don't make it back and someone else has to locate the spare weapons and ammunition. He gives me a look as if to say *you better make it back here. I don't care if you limp back, just make it back.*

I meet up with the rest of the guys at the staging area, a broken piece of road inside the wire.

"Which vehicle am I in?"

A friend who works in the motor pool as a mechanic replies, "Lead vehicle. You know that'll never change."

What the fuck is wrong with the commander? I think. Doesn't he realize the first and last vehicles are most prone to being hit during an attack?

Drivers and gunners huddle up for the convoy brief with the

commander. Everyone listens, because if you're not a driver then you're a gunner. No such thing as a passenger. Everyone locks and loads when we leave the wire. We complete basic vehicle checks, including radio, personnel, weapons, ammunition, and water. Once vehicles report good-to-go status, the commander orders the rollout.

We drive into Bagram, the town just outside the wire of the air base. We end up parking on a side street adjacent to a main road. The destination point is the corner building. We exit the vehicles and post guard while the commander and a few others walk inside the building.

Many of the locals, young and old, come out to talk. Most ask for food, water, even money. I stand with a firm stance and a look that says I will kill any of them who come too close to the vehicle. Sometimes locals rush toward the vehicles, trying to steal whatever they can grab, while others throw grenades inside.

When a young boy points toward my vehicle and little by little walks toward it, I tap on my rifle and signal him with my hand to step back, but he keeps speaking in Pashto and pointing. Kid, I don't know what you're saying and I don't really care. Just back away. Then the kid lunges toward the Humvee with his arm extended and hand balled into a fist. Fuck, he's chucking a grenade into my truck is my first thought. As he lunges, my M16 comes up to center mass, dead center of his chest. My finger wraps around the trigger a pulse away from squeezing. Our actions unfold in both a split second and slow motion.

Out of the corner of my eye I see his finger is extended. The kid's pointing at something inside the vehicle. He freezes a few inches from the Humvee, and I realize he's pointing at a Snickers candy bar left on the dashboard.

"Fuck, kid!" I yell, adrenaline flowing high and heartbeat accelerated. "I almost took you out for a fucking Snickers bar!" My finger unclenches the trigger, and an older boy, the younger one's friend or maybe brother, grabs his shirt to pull him back. I can't believe the commander left a candy bar on the dashboard. He had just briefed us on the importance of leaving nothing in sight that the locals would try to reach for and run off with. The danger often accelerates when a swarm of people start pulling things out of the vehicles.

I look at the boy now standing at the back of the group with a disappointed look on his face because he missed out on the chocolate bar, when in reality he was only seconds away from being blown into human confetti.

One of the other guards walks up to me.

"Hey, you okay?"

"No worries," I say. "I'm good."

He laughs when he hears what the kid was reaching for.

A few more kids show up, and among them is a girl about six or seven years old. She tugs on my BDU pants leg, head tilted, and the cutest little smile on her face. She reaches out her hand, palm up. She doesn't say a word, but I know she's thinking, please, Mister, can I have some candy? It breaks my heart to wave her away with the back of my hand, but if I give to her, kids will come out of the woodwork. A few other little girls show up and stretch out their hands. I wave them away too, and they wander over to the other soldiers. But the first little girl remains standing in front of me, smiling.

When I look up again, it appears the locals are rushing the convoy! I raise my weapon to fire a couple of warning shots when, through a break in the crowd, I see the soldier in the middle of the fray smiling and posing for pictures with the locals. You idiot, I think. We were given a warning and you're goofing off.

"Hey, bro," he calls to me. "How about a couple of poses?"

I squint in the sunlight and figure I might as well or he won't stop. I squat down, a couple kids jump in, and I wave the little girl over. Then my buddy snaps the picture. Before I stand up, the little girl puts her arms around my neck and gives me a hug. Because of my rifle, I only have one hand free, but I do my best to return a squeeze.

Moments later the commander walks out of the building with a couple of soldiers carrying cardboard boxes. He gives the order to load the trucks and roll out. I quickly pull a package of M&Ms from my pocket and hand it to the little girl. Her confusion over our leaving turns into a big smile. The other girls run back over, but I have nothing left.

"Let's go!" The commander jumps into the truck and closes the door.

"Hey, kid," I yell as I turn, reach through the window, grab the

Snickers bar, and throw it toward one of the little boy's hands. "Catch!" I see the boy waving the candy bar in the air as we drive away.

"What did you do that for? I was going to eat that," says the commander.

"No, you weren't," I say with a smile.

The following week we load up for another run to what I learned had been the meat and vegetable market. I load a bunch of candy this time in hopes of seeing those kids again. We pull up and park in the same spot as the previous week. I jostle myself out of the Humvee and post while the commander walks inside. Something doesn't feel right this time.

No people. No kids coming out to greet us. No one walking up and down the street. Just as I consider the reason for the silence, a little head pokes from around the corner of the building, hair shining in the sun. She smiles so wide when she sees me that I notice her little white teeth. This time I wave her forward with my hand. As I hold out the bag of M&Ms, I say, "Run, little girl, run. It's not safe around here."

Something in my voice makes her take off running across the street and down the sidewalk, and, I hope, toward home. The commander comes out and gives the rollout order. As we pull onto the main street, I look down the road, but she's disappeared into the silence.

Sergeant Jose Githens, US Army, served in Kuwait, Iraq, and Afghanistan.
MOS: 31S Satellite Communications Operator
HOMETOWN: Silver Spring, Maryland

I'm currently living in Lima, Peru, and taking college classes online. I married in 2011, and my wife and I are expecting our firstborn in December 2012. Soon after the birth of our child, we plan to move back to Silver Spring, Maryland, where I will obtain my bachelor's and master's degrees. I hope to work in the research and development of products and devices that provide a better way of life for all mankind. A couple years ago a friend and I opened a telecommunications/IT company, and I have been working from Lima. Someday, however, and this is a long-range plan, I would like to open a beer brewery!

DEATH THROUGH A 9X SCOPE   The desert air is stagnant in the peculiar L-shaped room. Old photographs of Iraqi policemen laughing, remnants of calmer years, lie scattered about the floor. "Should be a quick one," I was told in the operations brief. "In and out in a couple of hours. Just make sure that ASR (alternate supply route) gets swept for IEDs." Four feet back from the solitary second-floor window, my spotter and I sit and stare through scopes waiting for the sweep.

14:22: "Viper COC (chain of command), this is Thunder Actual. We are Oscar Mike on ASR Lincoln."

"Well, it's about fucking time! That was fucking bullshit, dude!" Luke, my spotter, has had enough of waiting games. We watch as the vehicles in the sweep draw closer and closer to the village, and the closer they get the more the village seems to come alive in a way that is all too familiar.

"Look alive, dude, the Spidey senses are tingling," I say.

"Yours too, huh?"

In an instant windows erupt with blossoms of gunfire all directed at the Marines of 1/7, my brothers. At once, the .50s and the 240s splinter the walls that make up the buildings of Karma. A call for air goes out, immediately followed by a broken but readable "Shadow 1, you are clear to engage all threats with positive identification."

I sit in silence for a moment. My rifle, covered with bits of sand-bag-colored spray paint to make it invisible to all except the man behind it, stares back at me. I feel the warmth of the bolt handle in my grasp as it slings back in the action. The 7.62mm NATO round slams into the breach, with the bolt locking behind it. The curve of the trigger, unlike the bolt handle, feels as cold as death itself. Aim, breathe, pause, squeeze, and BANG! Let the round surprise you. The vapor trail streaming behind the round lets me know it will hit its mark.

One by one the muzzle flashes are silenced by the barrels of machine guns and a sniper team. The Stinger missiles launch from attack helicopters, machine guns stack walls of lead, and in all the chaos eight rounds fire from an M40. A symphony of hatred and destruction composed against my enemy. The faces I will see in dreams were once people, but now they lie in haphazard piles of meat on the sandy floors of Iraqi homes. Blood pools in the center of each mud hut.

All is quiet now. A combination of pain and calm washes over me. Machine gunners have no direct targets, and Cobras never see theirs. But the faces of the battle-lost linger in the crosshairs of my scope. Radio chatter requests a battle-damage assessment, and a round-expenditure report interrupts my reflections. It takes a certain degree of insanity to walk into the houses of the enemy to do "dead checks" after a flying war machine has just laid into them with a barrage of explosive armaments. The evidence of human destruction is erased, and the bodies now rise as multicolored smoke to meet their maker. A smoke I walk through.

"Shadow 1, this is Viper COC. What is your RER (round-expenditure report)?"

"Viper COC, this is Shadow 1. I am minus eight, 7.62 NATO." Eight lives are gone. My hand shakes. I release the death grip with which I still grasp the headset. I cannot stop the visions in my mind. Machine gunners aim at a random target, a glimmer of light, or a semblance of movement, but then there are those eight rounds. Eight rounds fired at a face, a name. I lie on the second story of the police station, terrified.

"Hey, dude, wake the fuck up! Earth to dude. Paging Dr. Dude to the Humvee."

My eyes feel like footballs jammed into my skull, but I force a smile and load my gear into the truck. The ride back to the FOB is filled with dust and radio chatter. When we arrive, we find command pacing the motor pool, tingling in anticipation, aching to tell us what a hell of a job we had done, and that it had been them or us. We had done all the right things. I pick up my gear, grab my rifle, and fall into my can.

The night is warm. Wind picks up on the roof. After that twelve-minute tour of hell, I welcome the stale pack of Reds at my side. Hour after hour. Cigarette after cigarette. I hope for a flicker of light in my purgatory. As the desert sand whips across my face, all I can see is death at 9x magnification.

Sergeant, Anonymous Male, US Marines, served in Iraq and Afghanistan.
MOS: 0317 Scout Sniper

MY GREAT SADNESS I wake up to my usual routine of brushing my teeth and washing my face. I throw on my Marine uniform and head into work. Once at my desk, I check the time to make sure I call Trish, my wife, on her way to the office. I have two hours to spare before it's time to make the much-awaited call, so I head to chow with a few of the guys. When I return, Sergeant Johnson is parked on the phone, so I walk over to the Imagery section.

I call the 1-800 number, wait for the flat voice recording to begin, and, like I had done the other million times, I dial our home number in Virginia Beach, our home station. The phone rings and rings. Trish must be blasting music in the car on her way to work or has her phone on mute, as usual. I try a few more times.

Another twenty minutes go by, and I call her desk only to hear her answering machine message. By this time my mind spins with "what if" worries. So I call Lisa, one of Trish's friends at work. "No, I really haven't heard from Trish all morning, which is really strange," she says.

A few weeks earlier, Trish had said she was having headaches and couldn't keep anything down. I suggested she be checked out by the base doctor, but her stubbornness got the best of her. She put off making an appointment for a couple of weeks. Last night when we talked she had been on her way to the pharmacy to pick up the doctor's prescription. "Get plenty of sleep," I had said. "I'll call you in the morning. I love you."

Since she hasn't arrived at work, I call our house to see if she might pick up, but nothing. I dial my father. He had talked to Trish the evening before and knew the doctor had prescribed codeine to help her sleep. He figures that's why she isn't answering the phone. I feel sick. Something isn't right. I call every number I can think of over and over. Still no answer.

I walk over to my master sergeant's desk and tell him what's going on. I can't think about working until I talk to my wife. I can feel a fog slipping up into my throat, and my sight blurs with tears. I phone my father again to ask if he can stop by the house to check on Trish. I tell him I'll call him again in fifteen minutes.

"Her car is still in the driveway, but I knocked on the door and no answer," he reports. "Really, Chris, she's probably taken the codeine and that's why she's still sleeping."

I want to believe him.

Because my father does not have a key to the house, I call my mom's cell. I wait on the phone 10,000 miles away while she makes her way to the house. Finally, my mother pulls up to the curb, only to realize she has forgotten the key. I want to punch a hole in the cement wall. I wait. I sit in a chair with my face buried in my hands, heart pounding. When I again dial my mother, she is walking up to the front door.

"Hold on, I'm going in now," she says. I clearly hear the chime of the house alarm.

"Trish, Trish, are you up?" she calls. I can hear the stairs cracking as my mother takes each step. She opens the bedroom door. "Trish? Trish? It's Arthier. Are you up?" Silence.

"Is she there?" I say.

"She's here. Still in bed," she says.

"Trish, wake up. It's Arthier, Trish," she says. "Something's wrong, something's wrong," she repeats. "I have to call your father."

With that she hangs up. I am crying. The hands wrapped around my throat close tighter and tighter. I don't know what to do. I wait a few minutes then call my father.

"What's going on? What did Mom say?"

"I don't know. I'm on my way to the house now. Give me ten minutes," he says.

I ask over and over again, "What's wrong with Trish? What's going on?" He keeps telling me to calm down and wait until he gets to the house.

When he finally arrives, I hear him talking to people in the background. He's still not giving me any information. I lose it. I don't care who hears me or what I say. "What the fuck is going on? Is Trish okay?"

Some of the Marines have cleared out of the Imagery section because they know something is seriously wrong. When my father returns to the phone, his voice is calm and clear. "Who's there with you?" he says.

Sergeant Christopher Williams in his Dress Blue Uniform with his wife Patricia (Trish) Williams at the 2005 Marine Security Guard Detachment Ball in Helsinki, Finland. (Courtesy of Anthony Webb Photography)

"What does it matter? What's going on?" I say. "Is she dead? Just tell me!"

"Yes, she's gone," he says, still calm and clear. "I'm sorry, Son. I'm sorry" is all my father can say.

The world goes silent. I watch as my fingers unwind from the phone and the receiver drops to the floor. I fall to my knees and hunch over gasping. My eyes bleed tears.

Then I hear my mother's voice, far away, in the phone on the floor, "I'm sorry, baby, I'm sorry," she cries.

A surge of anger shoots through my body like venom from a snakebite. I storm out of the building, plowing through anything and anyone that gets in my way. As I blow down the hallway I hear a yell, "Hey, Marine! Stop!" I blow through the door as a hand grabs my shoulder. It's Master Sergeant looking to chew my ass. As soon as I turn I look directly into his eyes and at the top of my lungs with all the power left in me I yell, "My wife is fucking dead! She's dead!"

I run as far away as I can from that living hell of feeling. Standing outside under the pitch-black sky smelling of burning trash makes me more furious. I shouldn't be deployed. I should have been home with my wife. In bed next to her. There. Able to help her when she needed me. I am angry at myself for not having gone to college as we had planned, and I am angry at the Marine Corps for sending me out to the middle of nowhere. I rip off my Marine blouse and fall to my knees, anger still running through my veins. A few of my fellow Marines follow right behind me. By the time I hit the third punch, my captain grabs me. He hugs me and says over and over, "I'm sorry, Son. I'm sorry."

After several minutes a crowd gathers. I lie curled on the cement parking lot in a ball. All I want is to run as fast as I can home, across the sand, over the ocean, straight to my wife, my life. I hear the hollow, scattered talk of my leaders trying to figure out what to do.

They gather me up and walk me to the battalion headquarters so I can make phone calls in private. They assign a Marine, my best buddy, to stay with me through the night to make sure I don't do anything crazy. By the time I dial my father's number, I have realized she has gone. I ask him how Trish was lying, what happened. Was there a break-in? Was she raped?"

"She still lay in bed as if asleep," my father says. "The medics believe she passed in her sleep." My mother keeps apologizing. I tell her it isn't her fault and that I will be home soon.

My father assures me that Trish is being well taken care of and that the medics called to the scene were part of his volunteer squad. My commander comes by to give his condolences and fills me in on the plans to get me home soon. I am sent to the hospital to have my swollen, cut hands checked out and to talk to a psychiatrist. That night I am moved into another room, where my friend and I can stay until I can get a flight out. My other buddies come by and we play video games. They do their best to keep my mind off the events of the last twelve hours. We talk our way through the night.

The next day, the day I leave for my empty home, I open my eyes to an unfamiliar room and think the past day may have been a dream. Then I see that my sea bags stand packed next to my flak jacket, empty of magazines, and my rifle is nowhere to be seen. It is all true.

Sergeant Christopher Williams, US Marines, served in Iraq and Afghanistan.
MOS: 0241 Imagery Intelligence
HOMETOWN: Virginia Beach, Virginia

I am recently engaged and have a beautiful one-year-old daughter, Bruekelyn. I am still in the Marines and enjoying some downtime with the family while stationed in Tampa, Florida. We hope to get a chance to do a few years overseas soon.

800 WEST ASH STREET We live at the corner of West Ash Street and Seminole Road in a house painted the green color of faded money, and the green is curling off. The burnt bricks at the bottom of the house could hardly be called a foundation. It makes me sick at heart to look at the dingy off-white windowsills around the outside. If Gerry Thomas (a stuck-up guy in my class) ever decided to do a house inspection, he would tell me we came in last out of the whole first grade.

Once you actually make it inside the house, you might be surprised. My mother makes sure we keep it organized and neat. We kids have cleaning schedules. Each Saturday we're assigned a particular job. "Cleanliness is next to godliness," my mother says as she stands on the porch greeting us with hugs and kisses after school. When we first started cleaning and folding clothes, it took us two hours to get the job done, but once we got the rhythm of the thing, we cut the time down to just around forty-three minutes and fifteen seconds. My mother checks, checks, and rechecks our work. Then we run as fast as our legs will take us away from the house because to us it is just an eyesore. We play hide-and-seek for a while, or sometimes baseball. Then my mother yells, "Let's go, guys and girls," and we say good-bye to our friends and go inside for dinner.

One particular night, after dinner, my eight-year-old sister comes up with the idea of hosting a Diggs Family Ball.

She says, "I want you to wear a tie and hat. Make sure you brush your teeth, and oh yeah, bring some flowers and candy."

I say okay and go to the Holy Rosary Church garden across the street and grab some daisies, complete with big chunks of dirt hanging from the roots. Then I come back in the house and walk straight to my mother's clear-glass candy jar and sneak two Kit Kat bars. I don't have time to brush my teeth, so I steal a piece of Doublemint gum from the same jar. I can't tie a tie, so I hang the red, yellow, and green tie around my neck in a circle. I got the flowers, *check,* candy, *check,* tie, *check,* good breath (I hold my hand to my mouth and sniff), *well, good enough.*

Then I knock three times on my sister's door and yell, "Ready, my lady?"

She yells back, "Sure!" and swings the door open.

She has on her red-and-white Sunday dress with red, white, and pink roses as buttons.

"You look beautiful," I say, and she says, "Thanks."

She grabs the flowers and candy before I can hand them to her and throws the daisies out the window. Then she puts the Kit Kat under the mattress of her bed with the rest of her collection of candy. Now we are on our way to the ball.

Our route takes us through the kitchen and over the slippery tile, which is even more slippery in our socked feet. I fall a bunch of times. I stand back up and, boom, back on the ground. When I open the door to leave the kitchen, the room we are about to enter is dark. Now, take into consideration that I am only six and my sister is eight, so neither of us has conquered our fear of the dark.

She says, "You go first."

I reply, "You the woman, you suppose to go first."

"Are you scared, Sir?" she asks.

"No."

I take the lead as we creep our way through the room, tripping on the wire hangers and dirty clothes on the floor. This is our oldest brother's room. A few scratches later we make it to another door. What lies beyond is the living room and the venue for the ball.

I walk in first because My Lady wants to make an appearance. I ask the DJ to turn on the music (the TV). My older brother nods his head and does as I request. Then My Lady walks gracefully into the room, and I take her hand and we begin to dance to the sound of *The Cosby Show*. First, we slow dance, which is difficult for me since my socks slide over the wooden floor. As the night goes on, we continue dancing to the TV. The DJ switches channels to MTV and BET and we really glide.

About 8:15 p.m. my mother yells out, "Turn off that TV and go to bed, boy!"

"Well, we have to head home, My Lady. Sorry we didn't have more time to dance at the ball."

"That's okay," she says. "Besides, you can dance pretty well for somebody who wears Superman underwear."

I drop her off at her room, and then I go to my mother's room to tell her good night.

"You better get to bed, little boy!"

I try to climb in bed with her, but my little brother is already there. So I get kicked out.

"You got your own bed, Big Foot. Sleep in there." I run to my bed that I had never made up, by the way, and throw my dirty school clothes, candy, and old gum that I was saving for later to the floor. I'll clean it up in the morning.

I finally settle in enough to fall asleep when all of a sudden I hear, "Fire! Fire!"

A loud, screeching voice yells again, "Fire! Fire!"

Then my mother's yelling, "What fire? Where?"

My brother says, "Come on, man, we gotta go outside."

"Hold on, let me get my shoes." I'm in a panic fit trying to find my shoes and hat. Where's my shoes and hat? Oooh, man, Mom's going to kill me if I go outside without my shoes and hat. Ohh! What to do? What to do? The last time I went outside without my shoes and hat she had a fit.

Okay, I found one shoe. Now maybe I can find the hat. Yeah, look for the hat now. I got it! I can find two different shoes and take a shirt and use it as a hat. Then I should be okay. So I look deeper under the bed and find two different shoes. The shoe on my left foot is my Sunday dress shoe that I only wear to church and for formal events like school plays, etc. The shoe on my right foot is actually a boot that I used to wear when I went outside in the rain and I still wanted to play. Now what about a shirt? I go into my brother's drawer and dig for a shirt to wrap around my head. I reach into the drawer and boom! a fireman picks me up and says, "Come on, little man. I got you. Don't worry. You're safe now."

I yell, "I don't have my hat and shirt yet."

"What?" he yells. He looks confused as if he can't understand the words.

"Put me down, put me down, Mister. I need my hat and shirt." He totally ignores me.

"You big dummy, put me down now!" I start kicking my legs and swinging my arms to get loose, but he has a good grip on me. Then in desperation I say, "I'll give you some Kit Kat bars if you put me down."

He says, "Are you all right?" He looks at me like I'm some sort of alien. Then he walks over to my mother and asks if anyone else could be in the house. She says no and begins to walk my way. I see her coming but am too afraid to move. What's going to happen? Think! Think! Aw, man, I'm busted. She's going to catch me without my hat and shirt and punish me. She starts running to me and squeezes me so tight I can barely breathe. I'm thinking she's going to squeeze me until I'm dead. So I say, "I'm sorry, Momma."

She pushes me back. "Sorry for what, Pooh?"

"I just wanted to find my hat and shoes."

She pushes me back. "What, baby? I just wanted to see you again, baby. Don't worry about the hat and shoes or gloves."

Wow, I hadn't thought about the gloves.

"I'm just happy to see you, okay? Okay?"

Then my brothers and sisters and mother and I and a crowd of neighbors stand in the street watching the house burn. Everybody's hugging Momma. Some people stoop down and hug us too. Every object we own is burning. There is nothing we can do. After the fire is out and the fire engines drive away, my mother puts us all in the 1978 Pinto station wagon. We usually hate riding in it, but not tonight. All this action has been a bit much for a six-year-old. I had watched our house burn and burn and cried the whole time.

"Stop crying, you little punk," my older sister says from the front seat of the car.

"Leave me alone!" I yell between sobs.

My mother sighs the words, "There's nothing wrong with crying sometimes." Then she puts her hands on top of her head and begins to cry a low moan herself. Then we are all crying. My little brother is crying because my mother is crying. I am already crying like a little punk, according to my big sister, and I have no idea why everybody else is crying. We've been crying in the still-parked car for thirty or forty minutes.

I climb into the front seat and say, "Momma, you a copycat. You only crying because I'm crying."

She looks at me, wipes her tears away, and smiles.

"Well, I'm hungry," she says. "Y'all want something to eat?"

We all agree, and then my little brother pipes up, "How we gones eats? Yous ain't got no fritchen, Mommy."

I quickly correct him, "That's *kitchen*, not *fritchen*."

"Dat's what I said, fritchen," he says.

My mother laughs and cries at the same time. She puts my little brother in her lap and calls him her comedian. She takes us all to McDonald's, and we sit and eat and talk. Then we go to a hotel for the night, nestle in, and she watches as each of us falls asleep.

Sergeant Michael Diggs, US Army, served in Iraq and Afghanistan.
MOS: Information Technologies Specialist
HOMETOWN: Blytheville, Arkansas

BUSTED Wham! The door flies open, smashing against the faded green-and-black dresser, knocking everything over, pictures and glass cups careening onto the hard oak floor, old mail flying in all directions. She stands over my bed in a flash. I jerk around, almost snapping my neck. My eyes just about pop out of my head. She's in that red-and-white Bob Evans uniform with her apron half undone, short-order book about to fall out of her pocket, hat twisted, and name tag smudged with ketchup.

Her arm swings wildly. WHOP goes the first hit across my arms as I raise them to cover my face. SLAP goes the second hit across my back. SLAP SLAPSLAP again and again, blow after blow as she screams at the top of her lungs, "I thought I told you not to have company when I am not at home SLAP. How many times SLAP am I going to have to tell you!" With every sentence comes three or four slaps. "Do you hear me SLAP when I talk to you, boy, SLAP and the next time SLAP it won't be pretty SLAP." The hits come faster and faster, as if she is wound too tight. Oh, the pain rushes through every inch of my body. Please make her stop. Please, please, please, Lord, make her stop. Every hit takes my breath away. Please get tired of hitting me. Somebody help, please.

DISAPPOINTMENT Why, why, why . . . why can't you re-member anything? Why are you so dumb? Why are you so stupid? Who did your homework? What in the heck did you think you were doing? Can't you do anything right at all? Can you read? Can you spell? What is your problem? Go outside and play. Give me that homework. You don't know what you're doing. You can copy it later. You are just a big blockhead. You must have been dropped on that big melon one too many times. You don't know up from down. You will never be anything. You are a waste of space. Who taught you how to spell? You will never graduate. Why did I ever get with your mother? Why do you even try? You will always be dumb. There's nothing you can do. You were born that way. You're just dumb. It's okay.

You were born that way.

ONE MORE DAY   Beep beepbeepbeep. I fly out of bed, reaching for my pager while twisting the light switch to on. "Stryker Team. Go!" the screen reads. I gather my rucksack, weapon, NODs (night observation devices), extra batteries, and that trusty blade that always goes with me.

I drop onto my knees. "Lord, send your angels out before us that they may keep us from all hurt, harm, and danger. Amen." I never go on a mission without praying. I still hear pagers going off. I push open my door and yell, "Blue Team ready!"

We empty the hooch and run toward the Humvees with the six members of Red Team right behind us. Our team includes Red Devil, six foot two inches tall at about 185 pounds; Hammerhead, five foot seven inches, 165 pounds including gear; Smasher, the team leader, who stands six foot five inches and is 335 pounds with hands that look like catcher's mitts; and me, Silverback, five foot eleven and 200 pounds—just a little ol' boy from sweet home Alabama. We've been a team for the last nine years, and this is our fourth deployment together.

I got the code name Silverback after our very first deployment. We were en route to our target, riding through the black night, a few stars twinkling white. Red Devil, acting as scout, came running back to the convoy, fist thrown up in the air like a hammer.

"Small scout party," he yelled in a hoarse whisper, "heading our way. Fifteen to twenty men."

"Take cover. We'll take them in the path"—Smasher yelled the order.

As the guys took cover, ready for the ambush, I took off running fast as I could toward an old pine tree that you could probably put a size 5 dress around, petite little thing, and climbed to the top to perch.

Smasher on the radio: "Tenderfoot, what in hell are you doing?"

"Trust me," I said.

"Everyone waits for the signal!" he yelled.

The enemy moved in closer, and then right under the tree where I sat hunched in a nest of branches. I watched each one of them in my sights.

"NOW!" Smasher screamed over the radio while squeezing off his first round. The first ten fell almost in unison. Then another three or four dropped trying to take cover. I looked down directly at the top of the head of the enemy's team leader as he stood at the foot of my tree. He motioned to two men on the right to flank out and run behind our guys on the ground. They slipped over the bank and out of his sight, but not out of mine. I raised my weapon, picked them off one by one.

Only the team leader still breathed. He lay on the ground, weapon cocked, but as his men fell he jerked over onto his back and looked straight up in the air. He froze, eyes big as golf balls, a deer-in-the-headlights stare. His face turned white as moonlight. Pop pop—two to the head, and good night.

"Lights out," I said out loud. "Smasher, this is Tenderfoot. All clear," I said.

"Where in the hell did you get that move from?"

"I'm from Alabama, Smasher. All I did was play in trees when I was a kid."

"Hey, everybody, Mr. Tenderfoot has a new call sign—Silverback. He climbed that tree like a beast. I still don't know how that little old tree held all that weight."

"When I call your name, load up," Smasher yells in the present. "Here we go. Roll call: Red Devil, Hammerhead, Cobra, Worm, Silverback." This must be a big one tonight, I think, here comes Dark Night. He and Smasher talk for a minute.

Snake Doc calls out from the truck, "Gather 'round, men. Silverback gonna give us a prayer."

"Lord," I begin, "send your angels out before us that they may keep us safe from all hurt, harm, and danger, and bring us back safe. Amen."

"All right, load up. We have a two-and-a-half- to three-hour ride and then a four-mile ruck march. Let's do this!" Within minutes we are out of the wire and on our way.

Now in our situation, two or three hours seems like two or three days. Everybody makes his final check, and then most doze off for the rest of the ride. Time to clear the mind for the mission. Rocks pop and churn under the Humvee wheels, bounce us from side to side. Holes in the road seem to get bigger and bigger. I wander off. Just think, I started to get out after my first four years and move to Florida with my wife, but after the nightmares started, the plans, of course, changed . . .

I tossed and turned. Out of nowhere came the enemy. He was all over me, strong, determined to take me out. Not tonight, my friend. You're the one who will go. I gathered my fingers around his throat. He was weakening fast, panting like a dog.

"Stop! Stoppp!" I could hear my wife yelling in the background.

"Jessie, Jessie!" I turned to look, but all I could see was the enemy. The next instant, the bed, the dresser, curtains began to take shape. This was a bedroom. I was home! I was home on leave! I looked down at my hands in disbelief. My wife's neck was locked in my grip. Her face was turning blue! Oh no nono! What had I done?

"Baby, baby, I'm sorry. I'm so, so sorry. Please, baby. Forgive me. Oh, baby!" She lay dazed in my arms. What had happened to the sweet, gentle man she had once known, she must have thought. He never really came home after the first deployment, and he will never be back.

I returned home the next night from work to find that she had left me. So I am still in this man's Army.

Everyone sways forward. The crackling of the rocks grows louder as the Humvee slows for the last 1,000 meters. We're here.

"All right, let's go, guys. Double-check your gear and let's step it up. You got two minutes."

As I slip on my NVGs, I hear Smasher say, "Silverback, you got point tonight."

"Roger." That Smasher. Dammit. "Let's move out," I say. "Pick it up, everybody. Pick it up now. Double time. Let's get this crap over with."

As we move on, rocks smash and grind under our boots, and we're like a locomotive churning at a high rate of speed, steady in its beat. One mile done. Four to go. Then the ground's texture changes, and we make crackling, clicking sounds as we hunch up a slight incline for a mile or two. Now we're climbing. I examine every spot as if it contains something very important I have lost and cannot live without. Snakes and scorpions could be waiting to put their teeth in me.

Finally, we're at the top and heading down the other side, the dirt like grit sliding under our boots' every step. I try to stay balanced under my 35-pound backpack. I flop from side to side, gripping my M4 rifle tight to my side.

Once down, we move forward, a single-file row of thieves in the night. Reaching the village wall, I crouch to my knees. Slowly, with each step, I move closer and closer to the end of the mud wall. I am crouched now on my knees, my fingertips slightly touching the moist sand. I peek around the corner, scan left to right across the courtyard. Then in a blast of energy, I dart across the yard toward a rusty, mangled piece of metal, an old bucket and some wire. What it is exactly, I don't know. I plop down on my stomach.

"Smasher, I got one coming my way," I hear Cobra say.

"Stand fast, Cobra," Smasher says. "Get ready to take him out."

"Roger," Cobra says.

Swish . . . swish . . . swish. The sound comes closer and closer. Then a flash of light. Then the faint odor of menthol mixed with the musty stench of ass and six-week-old sweat. What the hell! I see a man's old tired ass sitting on that piece of rusty bucket.

All at once I feel the beads of sweat running down my face like somebody turned on a hot shower. Faster and faster—the faucet turned on full blast. I feel the ground sway, but it is only my heart beating out of control. I fear he will look behind the bucket.

Then he turns, and simultaneously I hear a quick poof and thump. A pot of warm soup splashes over me, and wham! I am staring straight into the half-blown-off face of the enemy. Cobra had taken him out just like that.

Smasher whispers, "Okay, let's m-o-v-e." I hold my fingers up: ONE, TWO, THREE.

We kick the door in. One of our team's right behind me, another sweeping each room as we go. Room One: an old woman, three small girls, and a boy who looks to be between the ages of thirteen and sixteen. Looking pretty good so far, everyone complying with the command to stay still. Then WHOP! and up against the wall I go with incredible pain to my chest and my right ring finger on fire. Wow, what in the—? Pop, pop, pop.

Dark Night runs through the door on the opposite side of the room. "You had a sleeper, son. You okay?"

I look at my chest, thinking I've been hit, but I'm only hurting from hitting the wall. "I'm good," I say as blood from my fingertip sprays wildly over the dirt floor.

"Cover them," Dark Night says as he whisks off with the others on the team to check the rest of the rooms.

More shooting comes from some of the rooms in the back. Then both teams reenter the front room with six male prisoners. Another six in the back had been killed in the shootout. Smasher gives Charlie Team the all clear, which means they can gather up the prisoners, along with fifteen to twenty vests filled with explosives, weapons of all kinds, and about 30,000 US dollars.

"Is everyone all right?" yells Smasher.

"Check. Although Silverback lost a nail," says Dark Night.

Everybody laughs for a minute. Just glad you're still alive, Silverback.

Sergeant Jessie Evans, US Army, served two tours in Kuwait as well as in Kosovo and Afghanistan.
MOS: 13P Fire Direction Specialist
HOMETOWN: Raeford, North Carolina

I was medical boarded out of the Army for PTSD, so I am no good to the Army or to myself. I can't be around large crowds, loud noises make me jump, and I have bad dreams all the time, so I stay medicated. I have been told that I am washed up and close to disgracing the uniform. I feel like shit, hate myself, and feel like I have let everyone down. Life is not good for me right now. But maybe someday it will change.

I WOULD RATHER DIE IN AFGHANISTAN "You are so ugly. You look like your ugly aunt on your father's side of the family. I knew I shouldn't have had a mixed baby. Damn, the older you get the more you look like them." My mother would say this so often I was surprised when she didn't. My mother would sit me on a kitchen chair in front of the window for hours while she parted and braided my hair. She dressed me like her little queen, black patent leather shoes and all. She thought such attention would change my features. When she was mad at my father, which was a lot, she would slap me for no reason. That was on a good day. Other days she wouldn't even look at me. That describes our relationship, which I thought was normal.

My mother had smooth, ebony skin, long hair, full breasts, nice round hips, a tiny waist, and flawless legs. My friends said my mother was cool and talked about how nice she dressed and the cars she drove. I made up my mind at six years old that she was disappointed that I was so ugly when she was so beautiful. I would look directly into her eyes and could read her mind. She was thinking, How did I have such an ugly child? My younger sister favored me, but my mother would say she looked mostly like her. My baby sister was by another man, but my father raised her as his. She was so light that I thought maybe her father was white.

When I was nine, my mother and father separated for a while. It happened during the summer of 1992. Then my mother met a man and was never home. By that time my mother had another child, my little brother. She left him in the house with me so much he called me "Mommy." I also watched my sisters all day throughout that summer. Sometimes I got raped by my older cousin. When we did see my mother, she was in a bad mood because she had to come home to check on us. She finally decided to take us with her to her boyfriend's house.

It was the worst place in the world. He lived in a crack house, but what made it so bad were his roommates, a very sweet crack whore and a drunkard that slept all day. Oh, and the boyfriend had

Sergeant Elether Fareaux completing a vehicle inspection of a JERRV (Joint Explosive Ordnance Disposal Rapid Response Vehicle) on Bagram Air Base, May 2009. (Courtesy of Sergeant Elether Fareaux)

no food for us. We ate dry Lucky Stars cereal without milk all day long, and, besides, the apartment smelled like sewage. Roaches crawled over every square foot of the place, which was filthy, and we had no hot water. My sisters and I would sit in the room next to one of the bedrooms and listen to our mother having sex: the moans, the screams, the bedsprings, and the headboard beating the wall. My sisters and I wished we could go home. My baby brother would cry just because we were crying.

One day my mother was mad at me so she threw me into one of the rooms. I thought it would be the same routine and she would beat me with the wide brown belt. Instead she threw the belt to the floor and gave me a look of disgust. "I hate you! I wish you were never born! You ruined my life! You will never be shit! You are so ugly that the only thing men will want from you is your body!" Then she turned and walked out the door. I stood in that dark room crying and wishing the same thing she did, that I had never been born. The crack whore came in and consoled me. She wiped my eyes with her hand and said that my mother shouldn't have told me that. My mother wasn't on drugs or a drunk, both of which would have made it easier to forgive her. She was just miserable and mean.

My aunt always told me that I would wind up pregnant because I needed love, that I would look for it—and she was right. She was a middle-aged black woman who didn't finish high school and had seven kids. They had all been on welfare since I could remember. My point is that she didn't need a PhD to analyze where my life was headed. She also taught me that the only way you settle with a man is if he has money and that most people could be bought.

What killed me about my aunt is how she could stab you in the back by telling someone something personal about you, and then come to your rescue in a time of need. How do you weigh that out? Stop trusting or take the bad with the good? Whatever man she built a relationship with wouldn't stay around long and didn't make her happy. To her they were sperm banks and ATM machines. She might've expected the worst for me, but I felt sorry for her.

When I started dating, I could see that guys liked the girls that put out. I didn't want to be labeled "easy," so I figured I would do the opposite. I would be the catch everyone wanted but no one could get. My mother had a reputation around the way, and I didn't want to follow in her shoes. It was now 1998. I was graduating from junior high and had a boyfriend named Greg. He was a good guy, respectful and funny.

Well, one day I was getting fitted for my prom dress, baby blue with white flowers on it, and he brought his cousin Daniel over. Daniel and I looked at each other for a few minutes and then away. Daniel and my cousin Tiffany started dating. Even though the four of us would meet at my house, Daniel and I always hung out to-gether. I guess Tiffany sensed an attraction, so she decided it was time to have sex with Daniel. I wasn't yet sexually active, maybe because of all those times I was raped.

Then Daniel and Tiffany broke up, and I broke up with Greg, but Daniel and I still kept in contact. Tiffany secretly resented me, which I found out four years later. Daniel and I had a connection that I never had had with anyone else. We did not pursue a relation-ship out of respect for our cousins. He was the only guy that liked me for me. Sex never came up in our conversations, and we never wanted to leave each other's side. He made me feel beautiful, and I was comfortable around him. He was my soul mate, but he moved, was arrested, and we lost contact.

My next boyfriend was a guy named Keron. Keron was from Trinidad and a few years older than me. Tall and skinny, he had very slanted eyes for a black guy. He was confident and the leader of a gang in high school, which I thought was so cool. I met him in the school elevator, and he watched me practice for the talent show. One thing about Keron was that he had a reputation for being a "cherry hound," which meant he went after freshman girls because most were still virgins.

Once I found that out, I decided I would be the girl he would not bring down. I was naïve. Then he told me he had needs, and if I wasn't giving it to him, he would get it somewhere else. He would take girls under the staircase and meet me after school with hickies on his face. When I paid an unannounced visit to his house, he was always occupied with other females. I felt like I should be grateful he would even talk to me. I was convinced I was ugly and didn't deserve him. The whole relationship made me feel like what my mother had said all those years was true and made my self-esteem worse.

The final guy I dated was a guy named Devon. He was from Brooklyn. I met him at my job, the cutest guy I ever met. Dark-skinned, pearly white teeth, long curly hair, and he could dance. The only bad thing was Devon was short, so if I wore heels, we would be the same height. My mother loved Devon so much she would give me money to give to him. When he got another girl pregnant, she begged me to stay with him. She said we would have beautiful kids. Other times she would throw it back in my face how stupid I was to stay with him. I thought she actually liked him in a different way than prospective son-in-law.

Devon taught me the types of relationship issues I would never put up with. While I was down South for a funeral, he hit on a few girls at our job. I was so desperate to keep him that I finally gave him my virginity. Like an ass, he told everyone I didn't bleed. I had never told him about having been raped. The truth was I was so used to being treated like shit by everyone else, so what was one more person? Then he gave me the line: "I love you, but I am not in love with you."

What made me finally break up with Devon was September 11, 2001. I was going to school late, as always, and had just arrived when I found out what was happening at the World Trade Center. The first plane had hit. Then the second. We were kept locked in the school. Then students started beating up all the Middle Eastern kids and setting fires in the classrooms. None of the cell phones worked, and police had to be called to keep students under control. Police even said we might have to stay the night in school. I was afraid and just stayed in my classroom at my desk. Later, I went to the gym and grabbed the largest bat I could find to protect myself. Then a few hours later we were released.

All the public transportation was down, and people were walking over the bridge from Queens to Manhattan. I decided to go on to work, which was near the school. I tried to call people, but freaked out if I couldn't get ahold of a relative. I tried to phone Devon for two days before I heard back. He came in to work on September 13, 2001, and I looked at him like he was a ghost. He talked to the boss, and then walked toward me. Said he was in jail on September 11th and was released the same night. I looked him dead in the eyes and said, "It took an act of terrorism in order for me to realize that you don't love me. Otherwise, you would have called me right away. Even if you cared about me a little you would've called just to say you were alive!" I walked up to the break room, tears streaming down my face. It took me two weeks to speak to him again, and I said, "It's over."

After Devon, I started thinking about what my mother had told me all those years ago. Maybe I *was* good for nothing but sex. Maybe I *was* ugly. I walked out of my room feeling I was worth less than dirt. My mother did hair, so she had a mirror on one of the doors in the middle of the apartment. I looked at my face as my mother's words raced around in my head. I stood in front of that mirror until my feet started to hurt. I asked myself what was so ugly about me. I had two equal-sized eyes, a nose, lips, a nice smile, not too much acne, and a glowing complexion. I touched all over my face like it was the first time I had really seen it, and, in a way, it was. I drew myself closer to the mirror and stared into my eyes. My reflection was looking into my soul. I cried like somebody had died. My mother was walking by and looked at me as if I had gone crazy.

"What the hell is wrong with you?"

I wiped my face but the tears kept coming. "All those years you had me convinced I was ugly! You had me settle for less than I was truly worth! Was it because you saw what you considered to be ugly, or because you were intimidated? Do you know what one kind word from you could have done for me? Do you know what I put up with because you thought I wasn't pretty enough? A mother is supposed to help a daughter through life, teach her how to appreciate herself, not damage her self-esteem. Look at me! Look at the mirror! I am beautiful! It took me seventeen years to see it! Look!"

Before I could say another word she smacked me. She smacked me so hard that my face felt fire red.

She screamed, "Stupid bitch," and I was crying, not because I was in pain. I cried because I finally understood what I was worth. For the first time in my life I stood for something.

The final confrontation I had with my mother was right before I joined the Army. She was dating some guy and got in a fight with his other girlfriend. I had just walked in from my current boyfriend's house. My sister pulled me in her room and said that Mother was in a bad mood.

I went straight to my room, but right then my mother yelled, "I wanna see that whore that just walked in!"

I went to the kitchen and said I didn't want to argue and that before she accused me I was sorry. She said I was a smartass, and I went back to my room. She kept screaming, which was normal, so I lay down on my bed while she screamed. Then a sharp pain hit across my chest. She was slamming me with an iron police pole! I couldn't breathe.

Then she struck again. I gasped for air, caught my breath, and twisted myself up from the bed so I wouldn't keep getting hit. I wrestled the pole out of her hands. She jumped on top of me. My mother's now 300-plus-pound body was sitting on my neck. The oxygen was cutting off to my brain, so I punched her in the side. She rolled off me but continued to hammer me with both hands, and then she banged my head into the wall. I didn't want to fight, so I just blocked her hits.

Then I said in a raspy voice, "You will not put your hands on me anymore. This ends tonight. I would rather die than live here another moment with you. Every word you say to me is what you think about yourself." I grabbed my book bag and a few clothes, and

I left. I graduated high school three weeks later and left for basic training the next day. The feeling stays the same: I would rather die in Afghanistan, in this war, or live on the streets, than go back there.

Sergeant Elether Fareaux, US Army, served in Kuwait and Afghanistan.
MOS: S4 Supply Sergeant
HOMETOWN: Harlem, New York

I left the military following my deployment to Afghanistan and now live in Dover, Delaware, with my husband. Adjusting to life outside the military has been challenging. I miss the security! I spent so many years taking orders that I find it difficult to choose for myself. I will be returning to college soon to complete my bachelor's degree in accounting.

A MOMENT OF SILENCE Today is just another day on Bagram Air Base. The routine is habit, and all I can do is watch the clock count down. I am contemplating leaving work early, but the consequences wouldn't be worth it. I stare at the computer in a daze.

Then I hear a high-pitched voice. "Anderson." It's Staff Sergeant Coleman. "Sergeant South has an issue with her promotion packet." Coleman's surfing on the Internet, and I'm annoyed because she's calling me to help the soldier. I walk to the counter closest to the door. Sergeant South, fidgety and perturbed, rambles on about three or four issues. I try to concentrate on the words tumbling out of her mouth, but have trouble focusing. Taking the packet from Sergeant South, I shuffle through the mountain of meaningless papers. The black scribbles on the documents dance around the pages in a jumble.

Then bang! A thunderous, deafening roar rips through the room, and the building shakes as if startled off its foundation. Then dead silence. Staff Sergeant Coleman crouches low in her chair, shocked and wide-eyed. Sergeant South leans against the wall trying to steady herself. I huddle below the countertop.

Slowly, I rise to my feet, walk toward the door, and grab Sergeant South's arm. She stares at me in disbelief. I sit Sergeant South in a chair and walk over to open the door. A cloud of white hangs in the air in front of me, eerie and foreboding in the night. Then another fulminating boom rocks the earth itself. It's a mortar attack, and they're exploding about 100 yards away. Mortars are a common occurrence, and I fear I will be the next casualty.

"Get the hell back inside!" It's Command Sergeant Major Showers. I am standing on the balcony directly outside our office door, stunned. I step back inside and slam the door. Command Sergeant Major Showers and Lieutenant Bonnell move to the main corridor along with the rest of us. They seem so calm and composed. After a couple of minutes, they return to their offices and resume work, but they have been deployed many times and knew what to expect.

Then the flight line comes alive with the rotating blades of helicopters. In the distance I hear the pop, pop, pop of small-arms fire and pray that the battle will soon end. A few hours later and all is quiet. As I put on my coat to go home, I hear Command Sergeant Major Showers and Lieutenant Bonnell whispering that there have been four casualties. South and I walk back to the barracks in silence, and I wonder whether the deceased soldiers were fathers or mothers. Had they talked to their spouses and children earlier in the day? Had they been scared or in pain?

I no sooner open the door to my room than my thoughts are interrupted by the rhythmic ringing of my cell phone. The voice makes my heart sink. The mortuary affairs officer explains that the team, which I happen to be a part of, is being called to unload bodies from the aircraft and is to be at the airfield in thirty minutes. I sit in astonishment, finally working up the will to put on my gear. I replay my training. This is no drill, but a real-life scenario.

As I approach the flight line I hear the low humming of the C-130. I try to soothe my nerves by imagining the moment I will see my husband, but I cannot overcome the knot in my stomach. The bodies are ready to be unloaded. I walk into the belly of the plane, and the stench of burnt flesh and boiled blood almost brings me to my knees. The black body bags are lined up in a row, and three of us take them down, one by one. I cannot see the bodies, but I can feel that not all are in one piece.

This day was supposed to be like every other, a repetition that I have come to hate. But as it turns out, the events of the last five hours will be etched in my memory. The soldiers who experience numbing routine are the lucky ones.

Private Emily Anderson, US Army, served two tours in Afghanistan.
MOS: 42A Mortuary Affairs Specialist
HOMETOWN: Bronx, New York

I am currently stationed at Fort Carson, Colorado, and living in Colorado Springs with my fiancé, Mark. Thanks to the Army's Educational Funding Program, I'll be completing my BA in psychology with a minor in criminal justice in 2013. I work with human resources while stationed in the States and mortuary affairs when deployed to Afghanistan or elsewhere. I am also the spokesperson for a crisis center for battered women. I encourage all women to stand up and share their voices, even in the most trying times. Whether soldier or civilian, your voices deserve to be heard!

WORDS UNSPOKEN   He stands in the shadows debating whether or not to take me. He almost did it once when I was a kid, and at an earlier time, when I was an infant. Death knows me well, but I have never seen his face.

Today it's over 100 degrees in the barrow pit located just outside the wire of what the military will name Camp Cooke, Taji. The "pit," as we call it, consists of four 15-foot dirt berms that we engineers amassed into place with our dozers. Our fortress is guarded by a .50 caliber and one SAW (squad automatic weapon) mounted on a 5-ton vehicle that would bring a tear to Mad Max's eyes. This is where I come to work, and this is where I come to play.

The local nationals, to be politically correct, bring raw earth in their Mercedes-Benz dump trucks and drop it in piles in my pit. It is my job, and that of my buddies, to sift through the dirt checking for UXOs (unexploded ordnance), IEDs, weapons, and ammunition of any kind, what we call "contraband." Then we load the dirt into our trucks and take it into the camp so we can spread it where necessary. It's a shitty detail, but the Army figures one or two of us dead versus ten or more in a blowup inside the camp is a bargain. Or, to be more practical, $250,000 versus $2,500,000 if you add up the SGLI (Servicemembers' Group Life Insurance), and the Army did.

It's closing time. The sergeant moves the HYEX (hydraulic excavator) to the second gap in the berms where the dump trucks enter the pit. At night this gap is closed off by a simple concrete Jersey barrier, and the pit is left to those outside the wire. I must hook and unhook a chain through both rebar loops on the barrier and through a hook on the bottom of the bucket so it can be moved, a twice-a-day routine.

Today, Sergeant sets the barrier in place, and I and another specialist go to work unhooking the chains. We are taught that complacency is just around the corner, ready to cause disaster. I don't know what happens in the cab, and neither does my battle buddy standing across from me, but I know Sergeant forgets to engage the safety lever, because I hear the hydraulics sing my impending doom. I stand straight up and yell at the specialist to move, move! But he couldn't have moved if he had tried. The bucket swings out too fast, missing him. Then it slams into my Kevlar, and I go down Goomba style, knocked down by the Mario of a bucket. No "100 points" sign pops up above my head. Death sprints forward, hesitates, steps away, disappears. But I glimpse the looks of horror as the bucket impacts the concrete rather than finishing me off. Sergeant says I stood right back up, and I believe him. It's just like me to act like nothing is wrong, but the impact with the berm proved almost deadly.

Two and a half hours later I wake in my cot with a migraine that will stay with me for the next five years, maybe the rest of my life the doc says. At first it is hard to move I hurt so much, but then again, it's not like I run from mortars anymore. Whatever the medics give me puts me back on my feet in just two days.

It takes my command a week to pull a convoy together to send me to Baghdad Hospital. A few months later, at home station, my battle buddies joke as we stare at the Safety Award plaque, which contains the date of my accident, on the newly painted wall and laugh. Sarge looks at me and says, "I fixed you!" The whole platoon bursts out laughing, because before that day I had kept to myself, and since then every other word from my mouth is me talking shit. The look in Sarge's eyes says it all. It was he who almost brought an end to me, and it weighs heavily on him. He is sorry. I smile back and say, "Yeah, you did." My way of saying, don't worry about it.

Specialist J. J. Saldana, US Army, served in Iraq and Afghanistan.
MOS: 62E Heavy Equipment Operator
HOMETOWN: Austin, Texas

I've had to put college on hold because of an upcoming deployment. I'm currently in training at Fort Leonard Wood, Missouri, and will soon be heading to Afghanistan.

FREEDOM I don't want to wake up this early in the morning, but my cousins are watching *Alvin and the Chipmunks* on TV with the volume turned high. I roll over on my twin bed to check the clock. Nine o'clock. I never get up this early on a Saturday. I am twelve years old, with no hobbies. I used to dance hula, but I chose to hang out with my friends Darla and Justine instead. I live at my grandma's house. The house has three bedrooms, one bathroom, and was built during the old plantation days.

The town is called Ewa, and it is surrounded for miles and miles by fields of growing sugarcane. If you have never chewed a stalk of sugarcane, you should give it a try. The field workers burn the leftovers of the sugarcane on harvest day, and the town rains black ash. My grandma has a garden of azaleas, lilies, and daisies all the way around the house, and the day before harvest we help her cover the flowers with old rags. Every Saturday my cousins Ben and Sylvia come over, and we go to the beach. I don't feel like going to the beach today, but my mom orders me into my polka-dotted swimsuit. She looks like she wants to get rid of me. She says, "Trina, you are going whether you want to or not."

When I get back my mom says, "Hurry up and get in the shower." I look in my parents' bedroom to see if my dad is awake, and of course he is sleeping. I am so angry at my daddy all the time. The whole house shakes late at night when he lets the screen door bang shut as if to say, "I been drinking Tennessee whiskey and what you gonna do about it?" And then the fighting goes on all night, with my mother crying. I daydream about a life without him.

I am taking my time undressing and getting into the shower when my mom shows up in the bathroom and whispers in my ear, "Hurry now. Hurry." I think this is strange, because she usually would yell. I still take a long shower. I run the water scalding hot until the steam fills up the bathroom. The hot water feels good on my skin after a long day in the sun. Once I get done taking a shower and I crawl into bed, my mom grabs me by the shoulders and leans close in to my face.

Staff Sergeant Trina Priddy sitting in a parachute sling in a C-130 on her way to Afghanistan, February 2009. (Courtesy of Staff Sergeant Trina Priddy)

"Do not say a word now, you hear," she whispers. She makes me get my shorts and a top on quick, and we walk on tiptoes out the back door into darkness. I am trying to acclimate my eyes as my mom whispers, "Hurry, hurry, hurry." Her hand pushes the middle of my back until it hurts. After we cross Johnson Street, she gets ahead of me. I follow, hurrying to keep up. My heart pounds hard and fast when I figure out we are running from my dad. I feel like I've been punched in the stomach.

It is late, and I am thinking the buses might be out of service for the night. If my daddy wakes up and notices we are gone, he will come out looking, and I don't know what he will do to my mom. I don't want my mom to get hurt. We reach the main road and see the bus coming, but it is going the opposite way from our direction. My mom says, "Come on, we're getting on anyway," and pulls me forward by the wrist. It is a safe decision, but the bus driver says his route ends in a few stops. My mom explains that we are running away from my daddy because we are afraid, and he lets us stay on until the stop before the main bus station.

We balance ourselves by grabbing the metal poles as we make our way to the back. The bus smells like Grandma's old perfume and sweat mixed together. I already miss my grandma and my favorite pajamas, which I have left behind, with a pattern of daisies bunched into nosegays tied with ribbon against a blue background. I have never been so scared in my life. My mom and I look at each other.

Staff Sergeant Trina Priddy, US Air Force, served in Iraq, Kuwait, and Afghanistan.

MOS: 3POX1, Security Forces

HOMETOWN: Ewa, Hawaii

I am continuing my career in the Air Force as an active-duty Security Forces instructor. I teach airmen ground combat skills by using actual scenarios from my prior experiences in Iraq and Afghanistan. What an amazing feeling to train new members in my career field. TSgt Richard "Smitty" Smith II has been my greatest influence throughout my journey here!

THE BIG BANG I grab my "bag of deliciousness," my snacks for the mission on which I am about to embark: some Girl Scout Thin Mints sent from home, strawberry fruit roll-ups, and the case of Rip It energy drinks I "acquired" from the DFAC. Then I throw my IOTV (improved outer tactical vest), with my Kevlar helmet attached, over my shoulder. Last, but certainly not least, I grab my M4 5.56mm gas-operated rifle with the ACOG sight (advanced combat optical gunsight) on top.

I dread this mission, partly because it is my turn to drive. Secondly, this is a "peace" mission, which means we can't be as quick with our rifles. I've been in Afghanistan, or as my niece calls it, "assghanistan," for a little over a month. I live just outside the city of Spin Boldak, a shitty town consisting of Taliban forces, drug lords, and people looking to harm us. I'm in the southern part of Kandahar Province, just next to Helmand Province, and the main border crossing from Pakistan to Afghanistan. Forward Operating Base Blackhawk is my house. Hearts and minds: that's the war we fight.

My twenty-five-man platoon is being sent to the village of Wanacka, 45 kilometers north of FOB Blackhawk. Today we're carrying rice, so our enemies can be well fed while fighting us; radios, so our enemies can have more components to build IEDs that can blow up under our tires; and news of our increasing number of patrols in the area, an effort to rid the villagers of Taliban forces. I drop my vest, Kevlar, and bag of goodies in the dirt when I reach the Stryker and unlock the Stryker's door and three hatches. I then move slowly toward the opening to the driver's "hole," a 4 x 3–foot steel-enclosed box of isolation. In case of an emergency there isn't a man who could even begin to pull all 275 pounds of me out of that can. I do a PMCS (preventive maintenance checks and services) on my truck: kick tires, check fluids, make sure we're good to roll. Then I set up my iPod on the radio box right next to the gunner's seat for the mission that will begin in twenty minutes. I drop the headset and turn on our speaker box. I sit in the back of the truck, isolated, not talking, listening to the sound of Lil Wayne singing "Go DJ."

Unlike most of my counterparts, I like to sit in silence before a mission, reminisce about what I have back home, a family that would love nothing more than *not* to bury their son, brother, uncle. I look down at my watch, check the time and temperature: 10:45 and 118 degrees. What the fuck? Then I tell myself it's a *dry* heat, as if that fucking matters!

"You ready, Mickey?" It's my staff sergeant, a.k.a. "Buck." "The truck good?"

I look at him with a sour face, as if I'd just put a handful of Sour Patch Kids in my mouth. "Roger, we're good to go."

He smiles, "Cheer up, asshole. I don't want a skid mark on my truck today." Staff Sergeant Ponzi is the one noncommissioned officer in the whole fucking unit who really gives a shit about his soldiers. He never asks how you're doing just to ask, he truly cares, and I respect him for that.

"I saw you in the gym yesterday and your max-out on bench press is the skid mark of the squadron," I say.

"Sorry, we can't all be Superman," he chuckles. Our platoon sergeant, Sergeant First Class David, calls Staff Sergeant Ponzi over to his truck. He is giving Ponzi the pre-mission brief, telling us the same stuff we already know. SFC David is in his fifteenth year of military service and on his first deployment, and here I am ten months in and already "in country."

I'm still sitting in the truck. Now it's "Z-Ro," a Texas rapper, filling my ears. Everyone else jokes and plays around. One of the guys has drawn a line in the rocks with the tip of his boot. A couple other guys stand, backs to the open ramp of the truck, waiting their turns to throw rocks at a pile of dirt in the motor pool. Others, like Russian and Beefcake, practice combatives by rolling in the rocks. Martinez, Juan 1, and Juan 2 stand around smoking and talking about the first foods they plan to eat when they get home. Then SFC David yells out, "Let's get ready to roll, bitches!" I grab my vest from behind the truck and throw its 40 pounds onto my shoulders. Then I lift it atop my head and squeeze my skull through the opening. I grab my Kevlar helmet, slip it on, and yank the strap tight under my chin. Time to climb up the side of the truck to the roof, take two steps, and descend into the hole, my prison. Once seated,

I grab the latch and pull it toward me. The Stryker shudders as the 200-pound hatch cover clamps down over my head with a thud. I'm in!

Once in place I reach over to my control panel, fire up the truck, and check all my gauges as I wait for the globes of my Caterpillar in-line 6 turbo diesel engine to warm up. Gas: good; oil pressure: good; temperature: good. The motor roars alive, an awakening beast. I pull on my headset and listen for the four other trucks, each in sequence, to call out their vehicle numbers, and then yell, "Redcon 1!" Slipping on his headset at the back of the truck as he stands up in his hatch, Buck asks, "Are you ready, Mickey?" I let out an unmotivated "Hooah," which to a soldier means anything at all except the word "no." Buck knows I mean "Fuck off" this time. He laughs and calls out, "Blue 2 is Redcon 1." SFC David's voice now fills the net: "Roll out!" I apply my foot to the brake while shifting the truck into drive. The turbo whines as I hit the gas and spins into motion 35 tons of metal, ceramic plates, and the souls of four men defending the liberties and freedoms of their nation.

"Sergeant Johnston, can we have the rollout song, please?"

"Working on it, Mickey," my gunner replies.

I wait patiently. To fill the time I reach into my pocket, grab my Skoal mint blend saved just for this occasion, and steer with my knees while I pop open the top. I slip an extra-large pinch of tobacco behind my bottom lip and savor the instant perk. I spit into the empty Gatorade bottle standing at the ready as Mariah Carey starts singing our song, "Bye Bye," soft at the beginning with just a touch of piano in the background. Then in unison all three of us join in from the Stryker: "This is for . . ." A funny sight: four grown men in Army Combat Uniforms—all of whom have killed—singing along to Mariah!

My metal beast roars along the narrow winding road to the single exit of the FOB. The gate, guarded by a skinny Afghani policeman and one twenty-year-old American soldier, is hardly a defense. The soldier pushes up the steel bar as the skinny Afghani grabs a rope and pulls it wide. I creep the Stryker forward, still singing, then mash down on the gas. We hit the 500 yards of moondust that has still not been plowed into a hardened dirt road. Damned Army engineers! My job is to make fucking sure we do not get stuck right outside the FOB. No problem. I pull up to the hardball road, one of only four or five paved roads in Afghanistan, and make the left to head north.

In a split second, Afghanis in white, yellow, and multicolor Corollas pull off the road to move out of my way. I think of Moses parting the Red Sea just for me. I slow down to a crawl, waiting to hear each of the vehicles in our platoon roar onto the highway. I jump the speedometer to 60 mph, and then I'm cruising down the road like on a Sunday drive. With the sky as backdrop, the distant mountains look like dolphins popping up out of the water. The guys and I have to laugh as Afghanis in front of us keep making those hard rights to get out of the way of us speeding Americans. So those Corollas *can* be used as off-road vehicles!

Then a warning shoots from the radio: "BOLO (be on the lookout) now issued for a handsome Afghani man driving a white or yellow Toyota Corolla." We all laugh in disbelief. Buck gets on the net: "Seriously, a handsome man?" Blue 4, SFC David, replies: "Roger, a handsome man."

We're on edge. Not because of the "handsome man," but because our superiors felt it a good idea to call ahead using their cell phones. Why not just call the enemy directly? Let 'em know we're cruising along this highway. We keep talk to a minimum. Our eyes search the dust on the side of the road for command-wire IEDs, which are rarely visible. The insurgent first strings a thin wire from one side of the road to the other. Then he squats down in the scrub ready to push the button and unleash enough explosives to blow us sky high.

Sure enough, I spot a fighting-age male driving a yellow Corolla. Buck sees him too. "Handsome man," he says over the net, "yellow Corolla."

"By whose standards?" I add. "He's only a 5 in my eyes!" We all laugh to downplay the fear of the handsome guy blowing himself up next to us. I hate when Sergeant Johnston is on my truck. He has a fucked-up habit of whispering ever so softly, "Boom." Every time we drive over a culvert or alongside a BOLO vehicle, a hushed, "Boom." We pass the car, and through my headset comes, "Boom."

"Hey, Johnston," I yell, "why do you do that shit?"

"Mickey, let me get a pinch off you? I left my dip."

He's the guy directly in charge of me, so I want to keep him happy. I toss the can to the back. "By your feet."

"Thanks." He grabs it. Before the military I had never seen a black man who chewed tobacco all the time.

"I'm throwing it back," he says.

"Just hold on to it. I already got one in."

"Cool," he says. "Remind me when we get back to the FOB."

We've gone about 15 miles north of the FOB to a town we call "Taliban Town" because of all the Taliban we've grabbed there. We call this strip of highway "The Green Mile" 'cause someone, although it hasn't happened yet, will for sure be killed here someday. I yell out, "GREEN MILE!"

The Mile is riddled with culverts, perfect for the placement of IEDs. A simple command wire run to a house near the side of the road would wreak havoc on us. I reach up, grab my Gatorade bottle, spit. This stuff is rotting my teeth, giving me cancer. What am I thinking? I came here with no expectations of going home. Made up a will the morning before I jumped on a plane for a country where everyone wants me dead. I left my few possessions to my family, decided who would get my truck, TV, Xbox, and current money, plus what I would get for giving my life to defend the Constitution. I picture my mom crying at the door in front of a man in Army uniform. Three days later the entire base shows up for a memorial for a guy they never met. They feel for the guy, and his family. He truly is everybody's brother. Unconnected in real life, yet connected because of the clothes he put on every morning. I snap back. This road is no dream. My life is on the line.

I examine every inch of the roadside. Buck keys up the mic 50 feet before the final culvert. "End of Green Mile" roars off his tongue. Sergeant Johnston is about to breathe out his soft "Boom," signaling we've made it, when I see a man in the desert wearing a bright white "man" dress and a brown *pawkul*, a flat, circular, haji hat. He stares intently at our convoy. My enemy wants to be clean when he meets Allah and his seventy-two virgins. My tires wind closer and closer to the culvert. I call out, "Target in the desert at ten o'clock!" I hear, because I can't see it from where I sit in the truck, the cupola turning as Sergeant Johnston aims his Browning M2 automatic .50-cal machine gun toward the ten-o'clock in what seems to be slow motion. My front tires whirl over the culvert that runs beneath the road.

"Oh, shit." Sergeant Johnston whispers. "Boom." Then the earth roars, "BOOOOOOMMMMM." The world goes black. I'm sittin' in the Chuggin Monkey with my girlfriend, Michelle, drinking a Shiner Bock. She's doodling a heart in the sweat on the side of her glass of vodka and water. She stands, kisses me, says, "I'll be right back," heads to the ladies' room. I watch as she walks away, her Coke-bottle figure disappearing through the swinging door. It's daylight outside. Light streams in through the window. I'm drawn to it, as if a child is tugging at my arms. When I walk through the door, I'm in a cemetery standing behind my mom, aunts, uncles, sisters, nieces, nephews, dad and stepmom, cousins, and friends I have not seen since I was ten. All wear suits or dresses. A casket, draped with an American flag, lies on a metal gurney. A picture of me in uniform sits on a small table to the right of the casket. A priest stands to the left. I'm dead now. No marriage. No wife. No kids. I try to maintain my military bearing, but I simply cannot. I'm crying like a fucking baby. I cover my face to hide the shame. Deep down there is still a little soldier in me.

I snap awake. My hatch is wide open. Buck and Sergeant Johnston are standing over me, on top of the truck. Buck yells, "I think he's unconscious!"

"What the fuck happened?" I mumble. They turn their heads toward me, bend over at the waist. "Come on, brother. Get the fuck out." Both men offer me their hands. I rip my headset off, jump up. An MK19 sends bursts of 40mm grenades toward a target. I gather myself. My truck is mangled. Smoke billows from the rear. I'm a ghost covered in white from the Halon system that extinguished the flames. I'm gasping for breath. My head pounds like hell and so do my ribs. I'm not dead! I punch the ballistic glass of my windshield and yell, "Fuck!" I grab my rifle. After all, I am still a soldier. I jump off the side of the truck, but I almost immediately crumple on the ground. The tires have blown off. The truck rests on its hubs. I try to stand. Martinez yells, "Lay back down, Mickey!" I look at him, dazed, and lie back. The scorching pavement burns my ass and arms. "You okay? What hurts?"

"I'm good, man," I grunt. "Probably just a concussion and some broken ribs."

"You lucky son of a bitch. We all thought we lost you."

"Yeah, I thought I was gone, too."

Buck and Martinez, the medic, help me to my feet. I look

around, mostly at my truck and the road. Two thousand pounds of homemade explosives can decimate everything in its path. Three tires were blown from the driver's side of the truck, along with the slat armor, steel bars spaced about one inch apart to stop RPGs from piercing the hull of the vehicle, thus blowing up the inside of the truck. The slat gives the Stryker the nickname "the birdcage." The mangled armor looks like spaghetti gone wild. The two-inch steel plate at the back of the truck, now twisted, sticks up through the floor. The mine-protection kit under the "hole" is bent into the floor underneath my seat as well. I am lucky to be alive. Lucky but unhappy. I must live through another ten months of people trying to kill me, which may make my dream of my funeral a reality for my family. Shaking, I walk to the medical evacuation truck. I can't wait to get back to the "security" of my FOB, where some Army doctor will help me "get better." I look around at my enemy, now lying dead after having had a belt of 40mm grenades launched directly at him. Thanks to a high-explosive round, his body was blown to pieces. My fellow soldiers, my "brothers," are each on one knee, weapons at the ready as they scan the desert waiting for the next attack.

As I sit in the back of the Stryker, I wonder what I had done to this person who now lies dead in the desert that made him want to kill me. I'm not a bad guy, simply a man who was sent to Afghanistan to help rid it of the people who terrorized my nation. But in truth, neither is my slate clean.

I still feel guilty for killing that fourteen-year-old boy as he wielded his AK-47. I had been in country for just over three weeks. I was sitting on top of an abandoned mud hut just outside of Spin Boldak. The boy was more than 400 yards away. He had no idea I was watching him through my thermal sight as he pulled security for his father, who was emplacing an IED on a dirt road. As I pulled back on the trigger, smooth and effortlessly, I felt the kick of the rifle and the crosshairs of my scope move ever so slightly away from his torso. I watched that 7.62mm round rip through his fragile chest like a knife through his paper-white shirt. His father was digging a hole, "planting" homemade explosives. He stopped, rushed to his son. I aimed the crosshairs of my thermal sight on the father's back as he knelt on the earth over his son's motionless body. I thought to myself, this is so easy. I squeezed the trigger back to the rear. Again, my M14 kicked against the bone and muscle of my shoulder. The round entered through the father's skull. He never even heard the sound. His body slumped over, landed on top of his son's smaller body, almost forming a cross. I knew I should not have felt bad about the family he left behind, a wife, other children. This man had been trying to kill me, my friends, my "brothers." I felt guilty for killing a boy only a little older than my nephew, a child. No more. Fuck these people. Die, motherfucker. Die.

Specialist, Anonymous Male, US Army, served in Afghanistan.

I plan on continuing to serve my country and my community by becoming a police officer. I am currently in college and looking to obtain a bachelor's degree in business management with a minor in criminal justice. I also do volunteer work at a local homeless shelter.

HE'S GONE   Playing with a child is like payday for some adults. Attwon, a clever young man, had the brain of Einstein. He knew the answers to the hardest questions and the solutions to most problems. Attwon was fascinated with the stars, galaxies, and planets. He would spend hours reading books about the Earth's gravitational pull and how long poison could be in a person's body before he or she died. Attwon enjoyed being adventurous. No matter how uncomplicated the game, he always managed to make it exciting. Tag could become an adventure in a matter of minutes. The typical tea party always ended up turning me into a magical princess whose servant was the faithful Attwon.

Attwon, a rather built man, had the strength of a bulldozer. There were many days he would push me on the swings at the community park for hours at a time. The muscles in his arm flexed with each push. Attwon's smile was as bright as the sun.

In Alabama the weather is very hot and humid. On a hot day, when there was nothing else to do, Attwon and I would fill up my swimming pool. Although his feet would hang over the outside of the pool like socks on a clothes line, Attwon spent several hours in my undersized kiddie pool. My mother laughed at the sight of oversized Attwon next to me. My mother never joined us in the pool, but she made sure we had a cold glass of refreshing lemonade for our outing.

I can hear him now calling me by my nickname, "Cookie Dough Batter, where are you?"

"Right here, Doughnut," I would reply.

As a child, the temptation of chocolate chip cookies for me was like water to a tadpole. Attwon, or "Doughnut," always had everything ready to begin baking in the morning. Rolling and forming the gooey cookie dough into balls always caused me problems. Attwon's hands were a lot larger than mine. My tiny ones couldn't quite get the hang of forming the soft cookie dough. Attwon was able to roll his cookies into a ball without a problem.

For some reason, I became impatient when it was time to put the cookies on the sheet. My small fingers would tremble as I helped move the cookies to the flat metal pan. Attwon had already set the oven to 350 degrees, and in a matter of moments the cookies would be ready. Fifteen minutes always felt like an hour. The sweet smell of fresh cookies and melted chocolate filled my nose. The day passed quickly when I was with my uncle. It would soon be time to get ready for bed, and I had school in the morning.

Glenda, my mother, always made sure her little princess looked fabulous and matched from head to toe for school. We didn't wear school uniforms at my school, so my mother was able to dress me as she pleased. My mother would spend an hour every morning doing my hair in several ponytails and making sure my little skirt fit just right. I think my mother ironed my clothes for hours. The creases in my skirt were hard as bricks and the collar of my shirt was starched down so it would stay.

After I got all dolled up, my uncle would walk me to the bus stop. I think Attwon knew the bus schedule by heart. He could count when the bus would come to the minute. After he gave me a hug and watched me get on the bus, I made sure I gave him one last farewell after I sat in my seat.

My days at school felt like years. I couldn't wait to get back home so I could see my uncle. As expected, when the yellow bus brought me to my stop, Attwon was there waiting with a big smile on his face. Seeing my uncle at the bus stop was better than cookies. Just to know that he would be there gave me something to look forward to all day.

Unfortunately, Attwon is gone. Air doesn't smell the same, and food has a spoiled taste. My heart no longer feels like a child's at Christmas with tons of presents waiting to be opened. My soul has yet to rest. I can now look back on those childhood moments and feel Attwon smiling at me once more. Although the cookies no longer bake and the bus has quit its route, Attwon still smiles. My heart is cloudy, but Attwon understands. Tea parties and kiddie pools are no longer part of my leisure time, and my mother no longer does my hair. But I feel Attwon's presence like heat in a cold room. Attwon is here, and he is smiling at me. I know Attwon lives in me, and I sometimes wonder if I live through him.

Private Eneshia Myles, US Army, served in Afghanistan.

MOS: 92A Logistics Supply

HOMETOWN: Enterprise, Alabama

I was recently promoted to the rank of E-5! I enjoy the military, which does not mean I can't wait to retire in twelve years. Currently, I am stationed in Mobile, Alabama, where I am also working on a degree in interdisciplinary studies through the University of South Alabama. My expected graduation date is May 2013!

ANOTHER DAY IN PARADISE Yeah, man. I'm thinkin', "There must be some kinda way outta here . . . I can't get no relief." In fact, I'm singin' my way outta this Army abuse, slipping away into songs of my youth while walking along in Mazerfa village, Iraq. This time I sing to the tune of Hendrix doing "All Along the Watchtower." It's 1330 Zulu on September 23rd. Ten American advisors from the 98th Infantry Battalion and the 5th Battalion Iraqi army are on a presence patrol. We're moving from house to house talking with people in the village to find out what's going on. Kids play in the yards while men stand in groups of three or four talking, smoking, keeping an eye on us.

People back in the States think we're all in the desert, but I have city patrol. The houses in this neighborhood back up to a dirt alley, and the yards are grassy like those in Ohio. Apricot branches bend with clusters of little green golf balls, and almost every house has a rose garden. Lots of cherry trees in bloom, too, with dark pink-and-white flowers. Most of the houses are stucco, a lot like ones in the southwest US, but older ones are made from sandy clay, and those are crumbling. Hey, one thing we don't have at home is the open sewers. Enough to gag a maggot!

And then I'm walking through a graveyard of abandoned Chevy cars. Why only Chevies? A skeleton of a fiberglass boat looks like it's growing out of the ground rather than sinking into it. Too quiet, I think. Kind of an eerie feeling. As we walk, we look into the soul of everything we see. We never know if some crazy bastard might be stooped along the side of a house waiting to kill us.

Too, too quiet on this block. Smooth and slippery, quiet as evening rollin' in. I'm movin' through yards, eyes wandering behind every bush, into ditches, over walls, corners of houses, in trees—looking behind, looking forward, looking down the road, up the road, listening to the excited chatter of Iraqi voices I can't understand on the radio. I look over at Salam, my interpreter, but he's already yelling. The dull moments don't last too long in Iraq.

"Sergeant Lowery! The Red Company is in trees. They is okay."

"What about Black Company?" I shout.

"They is on that side of the river." He points to the opposite side. "They is walking the river."

Hell, I don't see anything, but the radio comes alive.

"Spook, this is Rogue 6. Give me a SITREP (situation report). Over."

"This is Spook. The houses in Sector 3 are clear. Over."

"Roger, keep me informed. Out."

"Rogue 6. This is Rogue 3. Sector 1 is clear. We have some info on a name we've been looking for. Over."

"Three? This is 6. Meet me at the rally point!"

"Roger, Rogue. This is 3. Out."

I'm on my way to the rally point, singing away in my head again. Only this time it's Creedence Clearwater: "Two hundred million guns are loaded, Satan cries, 'Take aim!'"

No sooner do I have the rhythm going than I'm jolted back to high-pitched voices yelling at breakneck speed over the radio. Garbled Iraqi voices. Then shots echo from across the Tigris. My head snaps left, listening and looking for an answer from Salam.

"The Black Company is shooting from over river, other side," he says. "They don't see people. Just hear shooting."

The river's width is about half the length of a football field. It's as muddy as the Mississippi and smells like the sewers that drain into it. Some of the Iraqi soldiers, the guys on our side, shoot back in the direction of the sound. Pop, pop, pop, a burst of insurgent shots come back. Then, I swear, everybody's firing. Now we're getting busy. This is what we came here to do.

"Spook, this is Rogue 6. What's going on in your sector? Over."

"Rogue 6, this is Spook. Yeah, we're starting to have a little fun now!"

"This is 6. Yeah, give me your location. Over."

"Roger. Taking fire down past the mosque. I have Black Company and two of Yellow Company with me. Over."

I tell Salam to tell the guys to find something to get behind so they don't get killed. He yells into the radio and the Iraqi army guys take cover. We have a hell of a time of it. Bullets are kicking clods of dirt in our faces, knocking the damned bark off trees, and taking chunks out of the wall some of the guys are hiding behind. Nobody hit yet. Then all hell breaks loose. Two RPGs come at us along with a volley of what seems to be a million 7.62mm rounds from AKs.

I don't know what else was shot at us. The fear of death was running through our minds. Nobody was hurt. Later we got some intel that artillery rounds were buried out in a peach orchard. A couple of older Iraqi men gave us the tip. We came across a mound already grown over with grass, and sure enough, we found thirty-five mortar rounds along with a cache of thirteen AK-47s and gallon cooking-oil cans of bullets. That was the day! Like the country boy I am, I went right back to my singing. This time a little "Civil War" Guns N' Roses theme . . . we are the "young men dying."

Sergeant Benjamin Lowery, US Army, served in Iraq and Afghanistan.
MOS: 32B Military Police
HOMETOWN: West Branch, Michigan

I never thought life could be so wonderful! I recently married a great person. Unfortunately, I am currently deployed to Kuwait with the 3rd Army, Camp Arifjan. I look forward to returning home to my wife in Columbus, Georgia. Once home, I will be working with the Fort Benning Warrior Transition Unit helping wounded soldiers readjust to civilian life. I have been away from home long enough!

JOURNAL ENTRIES

5 May 09   Today is Cinco de Mayo. Not much to report, or is there? Yesterday I was awarded the title of Defender of the Week. I suppose I was awarded it because nobody else here takes any initiative. Since the 15th of April, I have amassed sixty-plus hours volunteering at the hospital. On my first day I changed the diaper of a man who is paralyzed from the waist down due to being shot in the spine. He also has other gunshot wounds. He looks American at first glance, almost like a pararescue or Special Forces soldier, dirty blond hair on top of a thin, leathery face. He had been a Turkish boxer. Apparently, he was unsatisfied with his wages, so the Taliban recruited him.

7 May 09   Justice takes many forms, but when I look at the scarred knuckles and battle-tested shins of the warrior insurgent reduced to what now occupies bed 6, I think it is almost other than justice served.

A little Afghan girl, about six or seven years old, sits outside in the waiting room. She patiently and silently sits, while sucking down forced oxygen from a tank into her small lungs. She watches me. Her eyes move with me when I walk in and out of rooms. Or at least they move with the weapon I carry, so I let her see me put it away in a locked drawer. There, it's gone. I slip the key in my pocket. She stares as if wondering, "Why? Why has this happened to me?" I feel sick, but I hold back any reaction and smile at her burned, charred face. Her little feet, which do not quite touch the ground, are twisted and burned too. Then I seize the first opportunity to turn the corner and bury my face in my hands. I feel ashamed of this. Thankfully nobody is around to see such a lack of military bearing. Work carries on.

3 June 09   I still think about how that little girl looked at my weapon—not invitingly, as with the insurgent in bed 6, but rather

Airman First Class Nicolas Gonzalez volunteering at Craig Joint Theater Hospital on Bagram Air Base, Afghanistan, 2009. Here he visits with an Afghani girl nicknamed "Razie" who was severely burned by an incendiary device that dropped white phosphorous on her village. (Courtesy of Airman First Class Jeremy Anderson)

challenging me to compound the injuries already visited on her fragile person. It makes no difference that the Taliban shot the rocket into her home and killed everyone save her father. There is no logic that a child can comprehend about pain this massive. Those of us who work in the hospital call her Razie.

17 June 09   Afghanistan really is another world. The climate reminds me of Cochise County. But the people are different. The men are male chauvinists. The women here have it worse than I ever imagined. A bride here costs $2,000. The males can have as many wives as they can afford, and marrying cousins is common. The average income here is $100 a month. Not exactly living the American Dream, but nevertheless here that is good money.

26 June 09   At the hospital there are many different wards that exhaust my volunteer hours. Of all places, I find myself most useful in the ICU. I am allowed to set IVs, do trach care, and everything from checking vital signs to removing and inserting catheters. The only thing I cannot do is hand out meds. I perform as one of the staff, not

only because I took one year of nursing and three years of anatomy and physiology, but rather because I truly enjoy the feeling of accomplishment I get when I physically care for the wounded and ill.

1 July 09   Today went smooth enough. Some new IVs and blood samples. Razie is becoming a familiar face. She no longer looks at me whenever I pass by. I was fine the entire day until I saw our new patient. She is a five-year-old Afghani girl. Her little body tells a horrible tale. The toes were blown off of her right foot. Her left arm is gone, along with her left eye. I found her sobbing quietly in her bed, as would a grown-up, trying to control her pain and fear.

6 July 09   I knew it would happen sooner or later. I was posted at guard tower Dealer 5 with Macnamee (the most selfishly depressed person here). Dealer 5 is way out in the middle of nowhere and perhaps the most vulnerable tower to guard.

The Taliban, however, were nowhere to be seen, and it turns out my enemy this night was an all-too-familiar foe. While I was being vigilant and a good airman, Macnamee was listening to his music on the new speakers I got off Kenny. Macnamee asked if I was done with my Coke so he could use the can as an ashtray. I said yes, and time passed.

I put down the binoculars and grabbed a soda and drank, that is until I felt the cigarette butt! Oh, man! The LN (local national) on duty with us thought I had gone crazy. I thought it was funny, when all was said and done.

20 July 09   I work with some LNs called green suits for the uniforms they wear. We learn a lot from each other. They teach me their language, which is easy for me to pronounce because I am Mexican. I teach them US customs. It is difficult for them to understand why I am not married. I failed in my attempt to explain the intricacies of falling in love and courting a girl, too. I told them that American girls are insane and that if they choose to leave you, by then they are entitled to half your money. They were awestruck and told me it would be easier to kill her! Radical logic.

Airman First Class Nicolas Gonzalez, US Air Force, served in Afghanistan.
AFSC: 39051
HOMETOWN: Douglas, Arizona

I have recently married the love of my life, Raquel! Woo-hoo! We live in England, where I work as a Military Police Investigator (MPI) for the 48 Security Forces Squadron (SFS) at Royal Air Force Station Lakenheath. I hope to return to my home in Arizona and retire on the family pecan farm with Raquel when all is said and done. Until then I look forward to applying the skills I've learned and have yet to learn, so I can be a strong asset in the effort of the US Air Force to maintain order and discipline among the troops.

FIELD OF FIRE   As a platoon sergeant for a forward support company in the 2nd Battalion, 8th Cavalry Regiment, I am responsible for the welfare of the soldiers under me in Taji, Iraq. My soldiers and I serve as escorts on what is called the route clearance team—Task Force Iron Claw, a team put together to find and remove IEDs from common routes used by our military convoys. We've been on over one hundred missions and have either recovered IEDs, blown them out, or had them blow up on us.

Our patrol consists of three up-armored Humvees, one Buffalo, and one Husky. The Buffalo is a large V-hulled vehicle. It reminds me of an RV because of the roomy cabin space and comfortable cruise chairs. It can also seat up to eight soldiers, who can move around and have good visibility because of the 360-degree windows. The Buffalo is equipped with a large hydraulic arm with a claw on the end for grabbing and cutting wire. The purpose of the Buffalo is to cut the command wire to an IED and pull it from the ground so it can be removed and detonated by EOD, a highly trained team that removes and destroys ordnance.

The Husky, which is designed to find IEDs, is also V-hulled and looks somewhat like a tractor. One soldier operates the vehicle, which is equipped with panels that work like metal detectors. The Husky has the most dangerous job of all. The operator lacks a crew-served weapon system, meaning he is alone in the vehicle. In addition, there is only one way in and out, which is the top hatch. On our patrols, the Husky always takes the lead. It is in front alone, defenseless. Husky drivers must crave the adrenaline rush of the job. No matter how many times their vehicles get destroyed, they ask to go on the next mission.

It is June 22, 2007, and we are traveling outside the wire on our patrol with the Husky in the lead, and then the Buffalo, followed by three Humvees. We are traveling to a small bridge with culverts on both sides, the same bridge insurgents tried to detonate with an IED but failed. The detonation cord made a loud popping noise, but the IED did not go off. Insurgents usually use culverts to lay down command wire to activate an IED. Bridges are perfect to place the IED beneath.

We travel toward the bridge, passing open green fields on our left. On our right, tall green foliage and lush vegetation run parallel to the culvert. The Husky stops short of the bridge, and the driver listens for the tone that signals the presence of metal in the ground. After ten minutes, the Husky driver begins to cross the center of the bridge. In an instant, an explosion at the Husky's position engulfs him in dark smoke. The shock wave rattles the ground and rushes at my chest like a hand pushing me back in my seat.

I call over the net to the Husky driver. I want to hear his voice. Know that he's still alive. No response. I call again. No response. I feel the worst has happened. In a panic, I call to the Buffalo driver over the net. "We got to get him out of there."

"No, wait," the Buffalo driver responds.

He's right. We always train not to jump out of a vehicle when a situation like this arises. The chance is another IED could go off or we could be shot. The enemy is always watching.

I call over the net to our battalion to report the strike. They want to know the damage, injuries, and whether the road is passable. How am I supposed to know? The event just happened! All I want is to get that driver out of the Husky alive. Another minute passes. No response. Damn, I hope he's not dead. How can I deal with that? Two more minutes pass, and the Husky driver crawls out of the hatch.

I receive a call from a staff sergeant with the call sign Cobra Red 2 from Charlie Company. They have the Bradley tanks to take on the enemy. "We'll be at your location in a minute."

Cobra Red's platoon is set up a mile back from our location. The gunner in the first Humvee sees a couple of black-hooded insurgents running from a berm about 150 meters at our patrol's eleven-o'clock position. He begins shooting at the insurgents and into the wide open field.

Behind our position I hear three Bradleys coming closer. Their tracks make a rattle-chirp-rattle-chirp sound, which shakes the hard-boiled ground behind us. Cobra Red 2 finally arrives with two other Bradleys. He begins shooting his .50 caliber. This continues for five minutes. The whole field lights up with small fires begun by the hot-tracer rounds that spit out of the .50 caliber, as well as the other weapons that are firing. The shooting finally stops. Cobra Red 2 calls over the net to me, "Are you good now?"

"Yes, thanks for the help."

He replies, "If you need anything else, just give us a call." The Bradleys' tracks rattle-chirp-rattle-chirp loudly as they make a 180-degree turn. Then the jet engines that power the vehicles roar away from us.

We finally dismount. It is turning dusk. The field is still on fire. I move up to the front to see the devastation caused by the IED. The driver looks a little dazed. The Husky is broken in half from the rear axle, and the IED took out the entire bridge. The hole created by the explosion is 10 feet deep and 20 feet wide! We take photos with two soldiers standing in it while we wait for a wrecker to recover the Husky.

After many such patrols I finally went on R&R leave. When I returned, I learned that Cobra Red 2 was killed the day I left for leave. He was at the same location where the IED had blown up the bridge. A sniper shot him in the neck.

Sergeant Jeffrey Lambert, US Army, served two tours each in Iraq and Afghanistan.
MOS: 92G Senior Food Operations Specialist
HOMETOWN: Elba, New York

NEW PARENTS DAY   I'm not sure why today is any different from those other days I got new parents. Every other time I got moved to a new house, the ladies in black told me those people were going to be my new parents too. But this morning the ladies in black seem different. They get out of their car, their black dresses blowing in circles like leaves on a windy day. They laugh, run up to the porch where I sit, and ask if I am ready. They laugh again and tell me they are really excited about today, and that today is the day they have been praying for, whatever that means.

Usually, the ladies would pick me up and drive me to my new home. I'd get to ride in their big shiny car with two rows of seats in the back. They would let me sit in the front seat. I had parents once that made me sit in the backseat while the other kids sat in the front. Those kids would make fun of me and throw empty candy wrappers at me.

But today, the ladies in black take me to the city. We stop at a building with big windows and pretty colored pictures in them. Little monsters sit on the corners at the top of the building, watching me. The ladies call this place a church. We walk into the church where monsters live. The ladies take me into a big room with pictures on the wall. They sit me in a big chair, which makes my feet hang in the air. "We'll be back in a few minutes, little man." They close the door and leave.

I look at the pictures of people with wings. Some have little yellow circles around their heads. One picture is of a man hanging on a tree. His hands and feet are bleeding, which makes me sad. The room has big windows and it looks like dust is flying around in the room. The ladies in black open the door. They set milk and cookies down on the table in front of my big chair. The biggest lady, who laughs a lot, tells me I am a good boy. She pats me on the head and says my new parents will be here soon. She says my new parents will take me to my home. They leave me alone in the big room with the milk and cookies.

I'm not sure I want new parents again. The last ones didn't like me much. They made me sit in the corner and watch them eat. They had two other kids who were real mean. They would beat me up. Sometimes I would hit one of them real hard. He'd cry and tell the mean big man that I hit him. I got spankings from the mean man. He scared me a lot. He would yell, take off his belt, and hit me on the back with it. The other kids would laugh when I cried.

The ladies in black say that I am going to have my own room this time, with a bed and windows. I had my own room last time, and I didn't like it much. It was also where all the clothes and shoes were kept. One little light hung from the ceiling, but most of the time it didn't work. It was so high I couldn't reach it anyway. I don't remember ever having a bed. I saw the beds those other kids had, but I don't remember having one. Where I slept, the floor was always cold. I would take the furry coat off the hanger, put it on the floor, and sleep on top of it. It smelled like the lady. I'd lie on top of it and watch the little light under the door. Sometimes shadows would move around in the light, but nobody ever opened the door when I was scared. Finally, the light would go out. It was real dark then.

The lady in the house was always sad. She cried a lot. Sometimes late at night when all the lights were out, she would come into my little room and wake me up. She picked me off the floor and took me to her favorite chair. She always cried. I'd sit on her lap and wonder if she had gotten a spanking too. I think she was a nice lady. She rocked me for a while and then kissed me on the head. Then she put me back in the little room with the coats. She kissed me again and pulled the string so the light would come on. I think she knew I was afraid of the dark.

I am still waiting for the ladies in black to return. The door opens. This time the big man that wears black comes in. He laughs and plays with me every time I see him. Sometimes he gives me a hug and lifts me off the floor. He looks like a big bear. I like him. He walks over to me and asks if I'm ready to go to my new home. He has white hair that snows a lot on his black coat. I ask why I can't live with him and the ladies in black. He pats me on the head and says this time I'm going to a real home with nice people who want to adopt me. I ask, "What does adopt mean?" He says these people are going to love me. He opens the door and leaves. I want to ask what "love" means, but I am too late.

The door opens again. The ladies in black rush in. They say my new parents are here. They say my new parents have given me a beautiful name, Jonathon. They stand me up and straighten my clothes. The big lady even licks her hand and rubs it over my hair. As we leave the room I ask, "What was my name before?"

The lady with the long necklace kneels down in front of me and takes my hand. Her necklace has the same picture of the poor man hanging on the tree bleeding. She says my name before doesn't matter. She says now I have a beautiful name, and it's mine forever.

They take me by the hands, one lady on each side of me. We walk down a long hallway. On the walls I see a lot of pictures again. And there are lots of chairs and a big statue of that same man hanging from the tall tree. We stop at the big doors. I see a bowl of water on each side. The ladies in black put their hands into the bowls and touch their heads. The biggest lady puts water on my head. I hear talking and laughing outside the big doors. Then the two ladies open the doors and the sun is really bright. I can't see anything. I hear the nice man in black say, "Here's Jonathon now!"

A beautiful lady walks up to me and says, "Hello, Jonathon." She bends down and gives me a box with a blue ribbon around it. She says it's a present. I am excited. I never had a present before.

Those other kids got pretty boxes, but I never got one. I look at the big man in black and ask, "Are these people my new parents?"

He walks over and puts his big hand on my shoulder. "Yes, Jonathon. This is Mr. and Mrs. LeMaster. You now belong to them, forever and ever."

The pretty lady tells me to open my present, so I do. It is a little brown bear.

Technical Sergeant Jonathon LeMaster, US Air Force, served in Afghanistan.
AFSC: 3E371 Structural Craftsman
HOMETOWN: Independence, Kentucky

My deployment to Afghanistan was the catapult that changed the course of my life. Although I still work for the US Air Force and am still a traditional Reservist, while on Bagram Air Base I continued my pursuit of higher education through the University of Maryland University College Europe. I have now completed an associate's degree in construction technology as well as a bachelor's in organizational leadership. I am currently enrolled in a master's program in vocational rehabilitation through the University of Kentucky. In short, I am living life to the fullest.

ROSES "Cowboy" made his living pimping women, such as my mother, who were in bad situations. He was smart. He got his girls out into the city by having them sell roses in nightclubs like the Blue Diamond and Crystal's Hideout. Every day hundreds of roses arrived at his house, and the working girls, including my mother, would spend their afternoon cutting stems, pruning leaves, and tying each rose with a satin bow. A sequined heart on a stick finished off the arrangement. At night in the clubs the women made contacts with johns and left Cowboy's number to arrange visits.

A hooker's three boys did not fit into Cowboy's business model, so my two brothers and I were treated as you might expect, locked in the dank basement for days at a time. The dusty light that filtered into the dingy room through the narrow, barred windows illuminated the drained face of my older brother, Kevin. He was ten at the time, but somehow felt responsible for us. We slept on a torn, cushionless couch or on piles of dirty hooker clothes. The ever-present roaches crawled across our torn shoes to nibble our toes.

And there was the hunger. On one occasion my mother took off with a guy to Florida for over a week. We were left with no food whatsoever. We could hear Cowboy's heavy boots pounding the floor over our heads, but neither banging on the locked basement door nor yelling until our throats hurt brought help. The first couple of days we ate ketchup and mustard packets somebody had thrown into an old refrigerator in the basement. And there were a few expired cans of condensed milk. We found a rusty knife under the couch in that godforsaken room, and starving, we banged on the can and then tried using the knife as a dagger on its metal lid. Kevin and I still share identical scars in the webbing between our thumb and forefinger from where our aim at the top of the can missed.

My mother had been raped when she was fifteen, an incident that ignited a powder keg of rampant drug use. I am the middle of three boys. Kevin is older by four years and the product of my mother's rape, and Corey, father unknown, is younger by eight

Sergeant Josh Wyly after patrol in the Garmsir district of Helmand Province, Afghanistan, 2008. (Courtesy of Sergeant Josh Wyly)

years. I never really had a man in my life who wasn't a pimp or a john.

Kevin and I had finally overcome the fear of being beaten by Cowboy. We planned our escape. We used the same knife we had stabbed ourselves with in our effort to open the condensed milk to unlatch the fly hook between the door frame and door that led to the stairs and then the first floor of the house. We finally flipped the hook! We were terrified. Cowboy was prone to violent outbursts. He had once whipped us with a wire hanger because we were making too much noise playing hide-and-seek in the house.

We crept up the stairs straining to hear the telltale clop clop of Cowboy's boots on the hardwood floor of his bedroom. We were starving. We held our breaths as we took small steps through the front room, opened the door, and ran to the house next door.

Kevin banged on the door. We could feel Cowboy's phantom hands grabbing our forearms and dragging us back to our dungeon. The lady who answered bent over our blood-crusted hands. I can't remember what we said, but she quickly took us inside and fed us chicken soup and sandwiches, and she phoned the authorities.

While at the neighbor's, we played with her son's Erector set as if it were our own. We were in a dream, playing with toys as though we hadn't a care in the world. We lay on our stomachs with our feet in the air like regular kids. But in an hour Officer Eastwood arrived. It would be the last day I would ever spend with my brother Kevin.

Officer Eastwood—weird to remember that name and yet filter out so much—let me ride shotgun in his cruiser while he drove what was left of my family to the precinct. He even turned on the siren for a few blocks and let me use his spotlight. Corey, my youngest brother, had not been picked up with Kevin and me. For some reason my mother had taken our little brother with her, an act I have never forgiven. Kevin and I were two filthy, malnourished kids with lice-ridden hair and stained baby teeth. In fact, I would not lose my baby teeth until age sixteen. I was later told by doctors that the body shuts down nonvital growth during periods of high stress and malnourishment. We were utterly alone in the world except for the company of each other.

Kevin would go into the foster care system at age fourteen—too old for a family to choose him for adoption, yet too young to be released. He struggled through several boys' homes and eventually ran away. I found him in a maximum-security prison a decade later, a rapist. Worse: his five children are all in foster care, just as we had been. Each of us makes choices in this life.

I have chosen differently from my brother. I am a Marine.

Sergeant Josh Wyly, US Marines, served in Yemen and Afghanistan.
MOS: 3211 Ammunition Technician
HOMETOWN: Austin, Texas

I am fulfilling my lifelong dream of attending Georgetown University. This is my senior year. I recently had the amazing opportunity to participate in a dramatic performance as part of The Telling Project, a conception of Jonathan Wei (see his website thetellingproject.org). Six veterans each first wrote a monologue about a dramatic event from military service, and then worked with a drama coach on delivery. We recently presented at the Library of Congress in Washington, DC. I feel blessed to have been surrounded by amazing people who have opened my life to opportunities I could never have expected.

MOVING ON   A salty mist rolls down my forehead as my duffle bags find their way outside. My plywood square of a B-hut room is now as eerie as a concert hall in the middle of off-season. This was the place I could go after a day of life on Bagram. The smile on her face made this room my personal heaven. A paradise.

I am ready to carry out the last box, the one that will signal my departure. Glare bakes the B-hut, but the room itself feels cold. My steps toward the door, slow. This box is heavy with a weight of its own, as if it too grabs on to the floor with hidden tentacles. Even my inanimate belongings do not wish this life to end.

The door marks the way from heaven to hell, mocks me, shakes with laughter as the wind blows. The glow outlining the edges hints at the harsh light outside. I am close enough to grasp the handle. Can this leaving be what has come of our commitment? I turn for one last look at the room.

Some say one can never go back. Faith tells me otherwise. I take my next steps out of faith alone. I will be pummeled with debris as I push forward. The door closes behind me, and I stand in a foreign place. The room, that mirror image of my heart, is as empty as a battlefield after the last of the warriors' cries. Bittersweet tears massage my face and cross my lips. Sweet for the memories I take with me. Bitter because memory is all that is left of my marriage. We made a pact to stand strong. She broke that pact. She broke me.

Sergeant Joseph Colvin, US Army, served in Iraq and Afghanistan.
MOS: 92G Food Service Specialist
HOMETOWN: San Antonio, Texas

I am currently stationed in Fort Riley, Kansas. At the moment I am working on reclassing to Civil Affairs or maybe Psychological Warfare. I have picked up the guitar as a hobby and use my spare time to teach myself songs that challenge my ability as an amateur musician. I've given some thought to writing a book just to find out what I have to say. I am married to Jessica, and we have a beautiful little girl, Kayli. They have become my life.

ANNA MARIA You know the place. The McDonald's on Muhammad Ali Boulevard. It sits back off the corner right next to Chase Bank. I manage that restaurant, and every morning when I open up, usually around ten minutes till seven, I talk to the lady that sits out front and buy the *Daily Tribune* from her.

Anna Maria, that's her name. Very pleasant and kind to everyone. She's my first customer in the morning and the last in the evening. She sits in a brown folding chair, always with a large cup of coffee with four creams in one of my cups. She is very specific about the number of creams. Anna Maria sits under the awning day in and day out in all kinds of weather, including the hottest days of summer and most frigid of winter. She smiles even during the rain- and snowstorms. They just don't seem to bother Anna Maria. And she is dependable. Even when she is not feeling well and has bottles of pills lying out with the newspapers, she sits in that old brown chair all day.

Over the last six years, I can't remember a day that I have not had the pleasure of seeing Anna Maria sitting out front. Most of my customers take her for granted. She is not the prettiest. She won't win any beauty contests, but she has a real heart for people. She always smiles for the kids. Her face lights up and she usually reaches into her purse for a sucker or a little piece of candy for them. Every once in a while I catch Anna Maria slowly getting up out of the broken chair to open the door for the older customers that have difficulty getting around. She is the Golden Arch good Samaritan. I get the biggest charge out of talking with her when I take her out a sandwich and cup of coffee, again, with four creams.

Anna Maria just turned seventy-eight years old. She's thin and frail, but she gets around like someone a lot younger. She will tell you that she is ready to run around the block if you are. Her hair has more gray than brown now, and when she smiles, you can see she is missing more teeth than she has. Her clothes and shoes are well-worn too. But in fact, I know very little about Anna Maria, and

I often worry about her as the years go by. I just don't know if she has family around.

Well, old man winter is here with chilling winds, blowing snow, and freezing temperatures that make you want to stay inside and enjoy the warmth. But as I open the restaurant every morning, the first one I see is Anna Maria waiting for her coffee and the *Daily Tribune* to show up. I just can't help but smile and admire that old girl.

It's a January day with the temperatures so cold it hurts the lungs to breathe deep. The ice crackles under my feet as I walk, and the sky is an ocean blue. No cloud in sight. The morning frost is etched like spiderwebs across the glass. I am running a little late for work due to the weather, but I notice right off that Anna Maria is not there, although the bundle of newspapers is at the door. After I open for business, I bring in the bundle of papers and set them up on a table with a cup so people can pay for their newspaper. All day I look for Anna Maria, but then I figure she is better off at home, nice and warm, instead of out front in the cold.

The next day I open my store, and no Anna Maria. Now I become a little worried. She hasn't missed a day in all these years. So again, I bring in the bundle of newspapers, set them on the table, and put out a cup. After I get through the morning rush, I find time to sit down and read the newspaper over a cup of coffee. On page 7, I read the story of a hit-and-run. Anna Maria was the casualty.

Every day I get a bundle of newspapers, bring them inside, and set them in a corner on a brown chair along with a cup with Anna Maria's name on it. It just doesn't seem right to have a red newspaper machine sitting out in front of my business when I have Anna Maria's memory sitting in the corner.

Sergeant Dan Yoke, US Air Force, served in Kuwait and Afghanistan.
AFSC: E391 Structural Superintendent
HOMETOWN: Parkersburg, West Virginia

I've been enjoying myself by building bookcases, cabinets, Adirondack chairs, and rocking chairs, both for adults and for children. I also build swings. I've never had time to open a furniture business in the past, but I hope to retire from the military this year to fulfill that dream. I enjoy spending time with my granddaughter, who is a sophomore in college. My wife and I also have another granddaughter who is ten months old and the apple of my eye!

ON THE SHOULDERS OF DEAD MEN I want to be a tanker. I want to be the tank, a depleted, uranium-infused, steel-plated titan of war. To crush my enemies, see them driven before me, and to hear the lamentations of the women. A tracked terminator in which the lords of battle would command me to leave kingdoms and republics both under my treads, to deliver resounding glory with menace, to instill such trepidation in the foes destined to cross my path that they would spew shit from their loins and quake in fantastical epilepsies.

Alas, you don't always get what you want. My recruiter, Sergeant Archer, says to me, "You're too tall for an Abrams (M1 tank)."

I take his word, as he is a short man. He shows me pictures of his days in the tanking field.

"See, those things are not made for your height. Trust me on this. You don't want to be a tall man in one of those beasts."

A day later I'm in MEPS (military entrance processing), San Antonio. With dreams of plated fury dashed, other options are revealed to me.

"Mechanized infantry," says the balding staff sergeant at the guidance counselor desk.

"Mechanized, you say?" A decade and a half of Robotech and Ultraman flash before my eyes. "Like, robots?"

"Ummm, no. Not like robots." The desk-absorbed NCO is obviously very tired of dealing with potential Army recruits today. "Mechanized infantry utilize Bradley fighting vehicles. You would either operate a vehicle or be a dismount."

Moving down the list of possibilities, he hits upon another option. "How 'bout airborne infantry? Paratrooper stuff. I could get you a contract for Vicenza, Italy. And a $20,000 sign-on bonus."

Cha-ching. "Sold." Outside, I'm as straight-faced as they come. Inside, my Spidey sense is tingling. I could settle on being a winged angel of death, leaping heroically from planes behind enemy lines. Yes, I could be an airborne something or other.

Three days before graduation from basic training, we're preparing for the battalion sergeant major to inspect the barracks, our gear, and our uniforms.

"Parade rest," the recruit near the door bellows.

"At ease! Men, listen up." The drill sergeant takes an uncharacteristic pause. "Someone flew commercial airliners into the World Trade Center." He stops, scans the rows of faces along both sides of the room before taking a breath. "We're going to war! Inspection is canceled."

I find myself sent to Fort Drum, New York. Never mind about all that airborne nonsense. Some things are not meant to be. After a few days I am assigned to a unit that already has a company deployed in the newly established War on Terror.

Weeks later, after many eons of QRF (quick reaction force) training and convoy security training, as well as tons of ammunition expended against foam and ballooned aggressors, we get word that our sister company, C, has seen action and taken casualties in Afghanistan. Our company commander, Captain Johnny "The Hand" Stevens, does the military unthinkable and jumps several chains of command to get us into the Afghanistan theater. A Company, Predators, contains some severely bored and well-trained units of light infantrymen. Discipline is tight, and the commander's creed is shooting bullets equals better soldiers.

So within forty-eight hours we are soaring through the night over the Persian Gulf and into the heart of Afghanistan. Landing at Bagram Air Base under the cover of night, all I see through my NVGs is a green sky above black mountains. First Lieutenant Andrew "Weapon X" Exum leads us by cracking a ChemLight, a glow stick that can only be seen through our NVGs. We follow him to our new home, a tent complete with cots sinking into muddy floors and a stovepipe heater.

After a little training, we're sent to a place called the Whaleback near the Shah-i-Kot Valley. I'm on the side of a mountain, a night sentry waiting for the cold to pass. Although more numerous in the sky than sand on an obsidian beach, the stars offer little comfort. Down in the black valley a firefight erupts. Rockets and tracer rounds fly in all directions, creating that Star Wars effect. It's the

Alliance (our side) versus the Taliban, as all armaments are Warsaw Pact weapons: RPGs, AK-47 small-arms fire, and RPK (Kalashnikov) light machine guns.

Slowly, like a burning forest fire, the battle moves across the valley floor. Then darkness, except for a slow-moving aircraft, a Valkyrie, cruising the valley like a servant of Odin who lays claim on the souls of the heroes, taking up the valorous dead with its infrared spotlight.

At 0425 I give the snoring Vato a friendly kick. I'll only get a half hour of sleep, but I'm not giving that up for nothing.

"Fuck you, Stock," Vato says. I slink back to our fire team's security position on the outskirts of our patrol base. It consists of a hastily dug ranger grave and piles of flat gray rocks. These Texas toes have never felt such mountain cold.

A soft crunch behind me and Vato's friendly cursing, "Fuck you, Stock."

"Fuck you, Fatty. See you in a bit."

Too soon the world shakes and rattles. I shake off a dreamless sleep with an aching vision of the cigarette I won't get to smoke today. The sky has turned a lighter shade of black now, almost blue. Beside me is Vato, Private Second Class David Vasquez.

"Fuck, Stock, you're slow."

"Your mom's slow."

Finally, the creeping ball of nuclear fission begins its ascent. We witness its photons reflecting off the mountainside adjacent to our patrol base. The deep cuts in the shadowed valleys twist and turn. Tan and pale-yellow rock and dirt. We wait in chilled anticipation for the sun's light and heat, a process that defines our concept of time.

"That fuckin' sonofabitch sun needs to hurry the fuck up," says Vato.

"Your mom needs to hurry the fuck up, but you're right. Why'd we ever leave Texas? At least back home the sun has the decency to show up on time."

Sergeant Lane creeps to our position. He is not amused by our amusement.

"Fifty-percent fucksticks," says Lane.

"And good morning to you." Another thing you don't take on patrol is manners. I digress. Sergeant Lane is respectable and knows his shit and can knock me out in one strike.

"Roger, Sar'nt."

Vato says go, and I don't waste valuable grub time arguing. I scurry back to the rucksacks located where half the platoon resides. Some shave, others heat MREs (meals ready to eat) or resign themselves to a cold meal. The finest breakfast buffet in the Shah-i-Kot Valley!

Soon it's time to repack our rucks and mount them again upon shouldered frames. We trudge up an ancient, dry waterbed, an uneven trek over small white rocks. Steep gorges rise up on both sides of the narrow path. Cliffs, really, interrupted by solid rock beds arranged in tiers reminiscent of the side of an Aztec temple. Only this tomb was carved by a long-dead river. At 11,000 feet the air is remarkably thin. We take labored breaths and swift breaks to adjust crushing ALICE (all-purpose lightweight individual carrying equipment) rucksacks by grabbing hold of our shoulder straps and bumping the rucks up while bending forward at the waist, conscious, of course, of the C4 (plastic explosives) and XM4 (experimental shoulder-fired rocket launcher; also called a "bunker buster") strapped to the top of the pack. Then we spend three to five seconds of desperate attempts to suck in breath. It's like breathing through a straw.

Every so often someone will call for a break. Who? Like I give a shit. I'm just glad I can throw this piece of shit ALICE to the ground and lie on my belly against a sun-warmed rock. But then I think of scorpions (I check my immediate area), coyotes, ants the size of cockroaches. Perhaps the altitude has had its way, as I see no life at all. There's a scene in the movie *Starship Troopers* where the platoon is ambushed by bugs, alien swarms that cut men to shreds. The book was better. I read it after reading all the Old Testament Braveheart stories in basic training. *Starship Troopers* was actually on the approved reading list. I think of the tactics of the Xenos, the giant bugs swarming the small platoon of infantry, and become depressed at our lack of robotic exoskeletons with shoulder-mounted nuclear weapons. What else could happen? The dead walk? Earthen troglodytes surely might just swarm from the deep caves beneath our boots. Either way, this gully is no place for a platoon of light infantry to be sitting.

On the move again, we meet up with 2nd Platoon. Everybody looks as tired and dirty as we do. They're moving down a similar cut, and the EOD experts don't look very happy at all. These guys are along to blow stuff up. Within minutes they are put to use when a very nervous sergeant hisses to our team's SAW gunner, Private First Class Butts, "Hey, dumbass! Move very slowly off to your side!"

Butts, who is only seventeen, is standing on a round plate 2 feet in diameter half buried in the Afghan soil. Turns out, you can stand on an antitank mine without setting it off, but the action will cause EOD (read: men who respect explosives) to sweat profusely.

We turn a bend and the valley view unfolds before us. It seems we might get some shade today, foliage and vegetation. And enemy bunkers. We're told that we're to clear and destroy all bunkers in the valley. We're pretty cheerful, the bloodthirsty, infantry type of cheerful, that is. See, we know we can shoot, move, and communicate better than our enemies. None of us are on a mission from God. None are fueled by righteous fervor. We are Predators, hunting our own natural enemy. While the Taliban have been in these mountains praying and watching shitty propaganda videos, we've been in Kuwait training vigorously, getting itchy trigger fingers, and getting bored.

Lane, our team leader, takes point. To the best of our abilities we form a wedge formation to go down the rocky slope. Butts is on the right flank, and Vato and I on the left. It's SOP (standard operating procedure) in our unit for the team leaders to walk point. As I understand it, when the US was in the habit of conscripting men, they would order the more expendable men to walk point. This is a different Army. Volunteers all. No one walked into these mountains against his will.

Lane is only three years older than me, but decades older in infantryman experience. He knows his shit and explained what shit he can do to us joes. His fire team consists of three very cherry privates. We're all fresh from basic training, and he's been working his ass off attempting to make real soldiers out of the mess basic training creates. The three months in Kuwait, when we were not shooting bullets, were spent in the front-leaning rest position, or crawling some inane distance over rocky and sandy terrain, or running over the same ground. And now we are here in Afghanistan, the foothills of the Himalayas, hunting those who would strike out against our cities.

Specialist Andrew Stock standing on the roof of the former Iraqi Intelligence Service building, in northern Baghdad, 2005. In the background is the Al Khazimiyah Shrine, a Shiite holy site. (Courtesy of First Lieutenant Christopher Sanchez)

The bunkers are everywhere imaginable, around every corner and under every tree. They're constructed of sandbag walls and wooden-beamed ceilings, covered by tarps, on top of which are stacked more sandbags—boxes with the textured walls of burlap sacks. Some are bigger than others. The smallest would fit one or two men lying side by side. Some contain broken AK-47s, video camcorders, and even bags of white powder, probably heroin. The larger bunkers, visible from the air, have already been bombed via the Air Force. These retain the stink of rotting bodies. Not even their sun-dried, martyred smiles hit as hard as the stench of flesh decaying in the open air.

When a bunker is assigned to our team, we initiate Battle Drill 5, which requires us to enter and clear. Essentially, we creep up to the back door and lob in a grenade. Vato and Butts hold local security as Lane and I approach our first bunker of the day. We reach its side and face the rear entrance. We crawl now, eyes on the goal. When we near the entrance and the good sergeant taps my shoulder, signaling action, I pull a grenade from the special pouch strapped to my chest, insert the ring finger of my right hand, and cradle the ball of shrapnel and heat in my left.

Back at Bagram, when the gods of logistics deemed our worth, they issued frag grenades, and we spent twenty or so minutes decorating them with various colored Sharpies. On the 14-ounce M67s, we drew symbols that cross language barriers, like smiling, poisoned faces, eyeballs and anarchy symbols, rainbows, unicorns, ice cream cones, heavy metal lyrics. One even wore the inspirational phrase "Eat shit and fuck AIDS chickens and die."

The grenade I hold in my hands is a gray orb with a blue spoon (safety lever) and a penis shakily doodled across its side. Now the spoon sails through the air, the pin curled around my middle finger, and my left arm outstretched, hand cradling a live grenade. I'm doing what's called "cooking" the grenade. At the end of my outstretched arm is a live, armed explosive device that could easily shred my team leader and me. One, two, three: I sling the ensuing disaster round the corner and into the bunker entrance. Boom!!! Two barrels enter the bunker doorway in a matter of seconds, but nothing greets us but kicked-up dirt, dust, and old shredded blankets. Deeper in we find a sleeping bag with Sesame Street characters that's torn apart like some crazed Halloween decoration and an unscathed video camcorder.

Somebody's shooting at us. I'm on the ground, crawling, following Lane as he crawls toward the small dirt embankment from which the shots originated. The PL, his FO (forward observer), and the PL's gun team are arrayed as a fire team, in line with each other, weapons pointed downrange toward a tree with a ditch beneath. A foot sticking out from underneath the drooping foliage provides the source of attack. Sergeant Hammer, our squad leader, takes up the flanking position and moves into point-blank range of the foot's owner and puts two rounds into him. The infamous double tap.

War has its rules. The law was told to us as this: If you pass a fallen enemy, it is illegal to turn around and shoot him, so be sure to shoot him twice before you step over him—the double tap. I try not to think about such things, since I've been assigned a hasty sector, which means we pull 360-degree security on the spot. We are each assigned our own field of fire overlapping our neighbor's to watch, and I lie down in the dirt, pulling security.

"Security" means go find some cover or just lie prone behind some rocks and wait for something to happen. The itch to turn around to see what's going on is maddening. Behind me Bravo team searches for the lone Taliban, or whatever the fuck he is. Before me lies a scramble of tan, white, gray, and brown rocks, along with sporadic patches of scraggy plants. Above, the bluest sky is punctuated by the local sun, high overhead.

I'm still thinking about the scene I have just witnessed. I think about the nice chaplain who held a pious chat with a roomful of trainees: "'Thou shalt not murder' is what the Bible tells us, men." I think he's Jamaican, but am not really sure. "There is a difference between murder and killing." It was at this point I stopped listening, even stopped reading the old Bible. Murder, killing, and annihilation are all semantics, as I see it. Pull the trigger, the enemy is neutralized. Success.

Bravo team removes grenades and machine guns from the Taliban nest. The gun, an M249 captured from a Ranger battalion that suffered casualties, is set up facing the bunker Lane and I have just cleared. Fuck me, I mumble.

"Yeah, fuck you, Stock," grins Vato. Our moment's jovialness is interrupted by Sergeant Lane.

"Okay, fucksticks, game faces, we're movin' out."

The next bunker we come across, Butts and Lane pull local security while Vato and I have the privilege of entering and clearing. We approach the bunker from its rear flank. It's angled oddly, with the entrance down a small hill and completely cut off from our over watch. Every bunker is different. This one has a stovepipe sticking out the top.

I silently pantomime for Vato to drop his 'nade down the pipe, as going down to the entrance would put us on an incline far removed from our local fire support. Vato removes his grenade and arms it and drops it down the stove exhaust. Only, it floats there. A pinless grenade at eye level is the last thing you ever want to be standing next to.

"Oh, shit! Run!"

I'm running and counting. At three I'm eating dirt and rock and floor. The grenade goes off, and then I'm rushing back to the bunker. Since the grenade did not explode inside, if anybody's in there, they are fully aware of our assault. Timing is everything, and I must clear this bunker. I'm at the corner of the entrance with my barrel ready to swing in. Smoke and dust pour outward. I hear nothing, and Sergeant Lane is calling for status.

"Vato! Get the fuck over here!" SOP is two barrels enter a doorway.

I'm yelling back to Sergeant Lane that the bunker is not clear. I steal a glance around to look for Vato. He's stumbling toward me, holding his rifle down with one arm, while his other hangs limp at his side. "Stock, I think I'm hit."

"What? No, you're fine. You just landed on it weird. Get the fuck over here. Two barrels, Vato!"

"No, Stock. I think I'm hit." He reaches me, and I see blood soaking through his sleeve. Shit.

"Sergeant Lane! Vato's hit!"

He responds, "Is the bunker clear?" I let off ten rounds into the smoky interior. Sergeant Hammer is on the scene with Lane. They're cutting off Vato's sleeve and calling for the medic.

I won't see Vato again until after we're back in New York.

Security again. My view this time is a crease in the earth that winds down from just below where I stand into a deep valley. At least I'm under a tree in this surreal world. If I were to suddenly hear a high-pitched beeping and find myself waking up in my childhood room next to an alarm clock, I would not be surprised, and I would definitely be relieved.

A day later I'm on a knee pulling security, waiting for a Chinook to pick up the platoon for return to Bagram. In a week we'll be flying back to Fort Drum. We'll stop overnight in Germany, and our company will celebrate heartily. Chris Butts will celebrate his eighteenth birthday by getting piss drunk and nearly missing formation in the morning. Our first sergeant tells us young joes that we don't know shit because we run out of beer once the bars close. We're not as smart as "Top" (our first sergeant) and didn't think to hide a case of beer in the bushes. That's wisdom right there.

THE HATE In my second deployment, a FOB in Kabul, Afghanistan, we spent long hours in watchtowers or on foot patrols around the small camp we were assigned to guard and defend. During this time I learned that the nature of reality and the cause of all suffering is desire. I set upon a path to free my mind from the binding chains of this illusory reality, or Samsara (rebirth or transmigration). It was easy to meditate and be at ease of mind, because no violence was being perpetrated against us.

Yet I carried a terrible burden. My oath to uphold and defend the Constitution was a barrier between my current situation and a life free of suffering. How could I foster compassion for my fellow human beings and at the same time ensure my M240B machine gun was accurate and clean, my ammunition coiled properly in the feedbags, and my crew trained and operational? I would walk the path of demons and give up hope of mental and spiritual liberation for my honor, as well as for the life debt I owed to my worldly comrades in arms.

A good friend, Sergeant Moon, asked me one day before we left for Afghanistan whether I would be able to pull the trigger. I had confided in a few about my realization that acts of violence only set us back, and that true liberation and peace would come through nonviolence and compassion. Men at arms do not care for true liberation and peace, I soon realized. Most only want their three hots and a cot. Upon taking my oath, however, I was reborn into a platoon of men at arms. I'll pull the trigger, Sergeant. Don't you worry about that. I keep my word.

Every day before patrol, I prayed that no target would present itself. I kept a tin bracelet engraved with the Sanskrit mantra *Om mani padme hum* (the mantra of the bodhisattva of compassion) on the buttstock of my machine gun. I wrapped a long sandalwood mala-bead necklace around an ammo can. "Keep my brothers safe and my enemies away from me" became a near constant mantra that I would repeat before and after meditations.

One night our four trucks are on patrol outside of Taji. The sky is clear and the stars crystalline in their perfection. A distant explosion, and soon after a call comes over the net that 2nd Platoon's patrol has been hit by an IED. One truck disabled, backup requested. We're en route before the order for us to move is even given.

The hit truck lies upside down beside a smoking hole in the road. An angelic, blessed Black Hawk is already flying away, taking the casualties to safety. Their patrol's leader, the platoon sergeant, is screaming mad. As he curses furiously into the night, a squad leader tries to hold him back, because he is fighting to get to the nearest house. "I know you're fucking in there! I'll fucking kill every last one of you fucking people!" The driver, Blakeslee, the fastest runner in the company, has had his knee destroyed. The gunner, Dawes, is pinned under the upside-down truck while burning motor oil boils the skin off his face.

A gray morning is in full bloom by the time we get orders to return to base. With dragging tires, we slowly roll back to the FOB. As we pass through a market intersection a mile or two from the incident, a small boy in a doorway slices his fingers across his throat, glaring at me. I dash all thoughts of compassion and freedom from this life of suffering, shatter them against the raging inferno. Hatred has me by the throat. Choking despair and churning fear all boil into one cataclysmic ball of loathing and pity. The tragedy of war is the realization that it would be all too easy to exterminate everything. I understand immediately how a company of soldiers could burn and murder a village. I understand the nature of hatred. Vile and corrupt, gladly does one put the noose around his own neck for a chance to strike out with murderous vengeance against those who would seize our cherished way of life and throttle the breath out of its lungs. Fear, loss, and pain are the bedfellows of maddening hatred.

Later, the bombs would fall around me, but I would never see a target of opportunity. Always the ghosts and the bombs and the craters, never a chance to let hot 7.62mm bullets fly. I would come to realize that the enemy is as hateful and murderous as we are. When crossing bloodied pools of former children or cleaning up the body parts of a voting assembly or finding a suicide bomber burning in his own failed contraption, the hatred flies both ways. Boiling, we stew in this cook pot of war. There is evil in the world, and it lies within the acceptance of war and violence.

Time passes and I find myself outside of the military. Home. Standing at a Valero gas station, a lone cigarette as my refuge, I find a shadowed corner to crouch in. I still haven't figured out what to do with this rage inside. A Muslim-American woman walks into the store. I try in earnest to stamp out this irrational racism I feel. It's all too easy to think of that village, that boy with murder in his eyes. The murderous intent burns you alive.

Specialist Andrew Stock, US Army, served in Afghanistan and Iraq.
MOS: 118 Infantry
HOMETOWN: Austin, Texas

Not much going on. I'm attempting to get a firm grasp on drawing from observation by taking a class over the summer. I've been taking workshops in memoir and screenwriting. My recent weekend at a writers conference made me wish I could sketch. Words fail at times to capture the whole picture, or maybe I'm not a good enough writer to get 'em right, but that struggle is the joy of writing, I suppose. I don't know what to say about myself in relation to what I've written for this book. I'm not ambitious enough to have any realistic dreams. Mostly I hope for an alien abduction, or at the very least, my own moon base.

Soldiers Tell Why Writing Classes in a War Zone Matter

PVT Emily Anderson, author of "A Moment of Silence"
Taking a writing course in Afghanistan gave me the freedom to vent, to speak out in a healthy way. The course offered an opportunity to interact positively with other deployed soldiers when there was so much negativity surrounding us. I made some friends—more like sisters—to whom I speak even today. The class gave me confidence in my writing. Class was what I looked forward to after dealing with the mortuary affairs team all day long. I enjoyed every minute of it.

TSGT Jonathon LeMaster, author of "New Parents Day"
In hindsight, I realize just how much my life has been altered because of my creative writing course in Afghanistan. It's easy to get caught in the trap of life, never pushing yourself outside your comfort zones. Dr. Leche, a.k.a. The Pied Piper of Afghanistan, and her class freed me from my self-imposed prison. Her song still drives my search for being more than I was. Thanks, Doc.

SGT Benjamin Lowery, author of "Another Day in Paradise"
Attending Dr. Leche's class was about exploring my ability to express myself through writing. I learned how to say, in words, some of what I have seen in my life. Not even a camera can capture the nuances of experience. I am waiting for my next mission to begin, which will be to work in the Wounded Warrior Program at Fort Benning; hopefully, I can encourage other soldiers and veterans to write as a way of healing and coping with difficult experiences. Writing is an important tool for me in deciding where to go from here and *how* to go from here. Some of the other students in Afghanistan saw our creative writing class as time away from the military and an important break in the routine. In a war zone we all think about those we love and miss. Writing helps with the sadness, the stress, and the exhaustion of being deployed.

PVT Eneshia Myles, author of "He's Gone"
Taking classes in Afghanistan gave me an opportunity to continue my education while in a war zone. Doc Leche is very devoted and caring.

Although life for a soldier in Afghanistan is tough, I'm thankful that I had the opportunity to attend college classes while deployed. The classroom felt like home.

SPC Chantal Ogaldez, author of "Spring"
Taking a writing class downrange was very special to me. It helped me to unearth many suppressed feelings. For those couple hours, I was somewhere else.

SGT Latayna Orama, author of "The Hardest Good-bye"
While deployed, it seems as if your personal life stops while everything around you doubles in speed. The opportunity to take a creative writing class gave me the chance to freeze time and make time slave to my every command. Writing is an outlet for me. I can be whoever and wherever I desire with just the stroke of a pen. There is a freeing nature to writing, and no matter how stranded or isolated I felt downrange, expressing my emotions on paper always loosened my mind from captivity. Deployed soldiers deal with stress and anger in different ways—some good and some bad—but I am forever grateful for being able to express myself in a positive manner. Doing so not only helped me on a personal level, but in my professional life as well.

SPC Andrew Stock, author of "On the Shoulders of Dead Men" and "The Hate"
I realized that the best feeling for me is the thrill of a fulfilling paragraph or two. When whole chapters come together I get really excited and pace around my house or step outside and let the world return to its normal spin. I'm going to keep taking writing classes till they kick me out or I run out of GI Bill money, but I know that beyond a classroom I can never stop writing now. I never realized how unfulfilled my life was until I experienced the exhilaration of adequately expressing the slow, gigantic stomping that I call thought into an actual understandable statement.

On Teaching Writing to Soldiers and Veterans

The terrain is harsh—plateaus and deserts, rugged mountains, dry open plains. The wind blows with unprecedented violence. But it is the uncertainty of man-made events, such as the rockets and mortars ripping into the supposedly safe zones of military camps, that keeps even those who live within the concertina wire on edge. In need of diversion, groups of soldiers gather in whatever vacant rooms can be found for creative writing and English classes.

They open the plywood door to the B-hut that serves as a classroom on this particular night. Desert combat boots thump across the gray tiled floor. Each soldier places an M16 upright into a primitive pine gun rack. Army, Air Force, Marines, Navy—the minutes leading up to class are a noisy clutter of war talk and home talk. These deployed men and women have little inhibition about writing what they live or what they left behind. War is immersion into the senses, the sound of an F-16 roaring up the runway in the middle of the night, the smell and vibration of a mortar attack, the taste of a rocket erupting a quarter mile away. War makes good story.

But on the first night of our creative writing or English class, my student-soldiers would typically do all they could to excuse themselves from the expectation they would be "writers." The range of comments would include, "Yeah, needed this credit for my associate's degree," "Nothing else to take," "Hell, tired of playing video games," or "Only other thing offered is math." They made excuses and joked, the way soldiers do before going to battle. Few had ever written for outside readers, whether about personal experience or, in the case of research papers, for academic correctness. To the young specialists and privates, the pen often seemed more intimidating than the sword. But as always they took up arms with passion and conviction. "I did my hell's best," was what they often said.

Think what it takes to produce a research paper in a war zone, with so little personal time, stressful living conditions, urgent calls to duty, few available computers and printers, and then the continual frustrations of frequently dropped computer connections, or, say, of locating an ideal source for a paper, only to have the screen freeze and then blacken. Yet their final papers, both in depth of research and correctness, were equal in quality to those written by civilian students in college classes back home.

During our first meeting, in both creative writing and English classes, I showed my student-soldiers the National Endowment of the Arts video *Operation Homecoming: Writing the Wartime Experience*. The accompanying collection of soldiers' writings was also one of our course texts. Against the guttural roar of C-130s and the *wup, wup, wup* of helicopters lifting up from the runway only 75 yards away, the film carried an immediacy and poignancy impossible to describe. Student-soldiers were mesmerized by the dramatization of other soldiers' stories that were so similar to their own. They listened with fervor to men and women "just like them" not only talk about their own creative writing process but describe their reactions to the fear, terror, angst, boredom, uncertainty—and definitely the humor—that make up the stew of emotions all soldiers negotiate while deployed. Written across their faces I read, "Hey, somebody captured the whole damned thing!"

The second night of class I handed out copies of Tim O'Brien's "The Things They Carried." I shared with them O'Brien's quote "The thing about remembering is that you don't forget," making the case that writing is remembering of the highest order. Writing records not only the facts, which we may or may not remember, but the emotional truth. My students gave this idea some thought, and after reading O'Brien's piece they were convinced: creating personal history is necessary.

My students in Afghanistan read a good deal of work by other professional writers who have been to war: Brian Turner, Yusef Komunyakaa, Ernest Hemingway, Joseph Heller. Introducing them to these "brothers" was an effort to reinforce the idea that real soldiers *do* write. By no means did I require my students to write about their deployment experiences; yet day-to-day life against the backdrop of war made conflict their theme, whether acknowledged, by default, or by omission.

The first writing assignment of the semester in creative writing classes focused on monologue, a form natural to them, since soldiers have a good deal to rant about: sleeping quarters, food, a spouse's infidelity back home, a recent mission, the lack of money to pay the mortgage in Monroe, Louisiana. They rolled it all out on the page.

Some raged about their childhoods, the other unresolved "war" many seek to better understand.

The rooms we called classrooms were often miserably uncomfortable. They were too cold, hot, cramped, noisy, windowless. We even at times sat on the floor in a sand-colored tent. And insurgent efforts to breach the safety of the concertina wire were ongoing, with suicide bombers at the front gate and mortars and rockets whizzing to random destinations. This was true especially in FOB Salerno, where my student-soldiers and I met in a bunker the size of a small room. But despite the threats and discomforts, our classes were spaces of intellectual freedom and light, time outside the perimeters set by the military. In the classroom students could be themselves, which meant the amalgam of identities that war demands: both the tough soldier and the homesick, lonely, tired, worried husband, wife, mother, father, brother, sister, friend. We were a microcosm of identities, emotions, and ideas within the regimented, prescribed, military confines of the camp.

Soldiers wrote dialogues, personal narratives, fictional narratives. Their senses worked overtime to record what could not be fully captured. They staked out their thoughts with abandon, pens silenced only by the greatest of human horrors. The young soldier's ink failed, for example, in an effort to write the story of a small Afghani girl who was burned over 40 percent of her body, including her face, when the Taliban dropped white phosphorus on her village home. The child, nicknamed "Razie" by the hospital staff, had been flown to Craig Joint Theater Hospital on Bagram Air Base by US Air Force medevac. Doctors attempted to remove the fragments lodged deep in her tissue and next to bone, but with each incision, the phosphorus burst into flame. Razie had also suffered deep wounds to one leg. But she survived, and as she healed she became a favorite of the medical staff. However, as in so many cases, the patient's release from the hospital still proved troubling for all who had helped her. Because substantial areas of scar tissue covered the child's face, back, legs, and feet, Razie lacked sufficient pores to effectively cool her body during the upcoming summer of 115–120-degree temperatures. Would she make it? Such were the preoccupations of my student-soldiers.

Many of our returning veterans have been sent on multiple deployments to Iraq and Afghanistan, and thus have compiled a history of their own losses: a friend in combat, a marriage, their own pre-war innocence, and their identity as soldier. Veterans speak about their military experiences, even difficult ones, with longing for that other self in uniform. Most dramatically, they have lost the camaraderie of others with like experiences, a brotherhood and sisterhood of understanding. Those with whom they shared the most intense moments of their lives are now scattered across the country or, if still in the military, across the globe, which adds to feelings of loneliness and isolation. A student-veteran in a recent English 101 class of mine at Austin Community College mentioned that he and two infantry buddies decided to move to Austin and share an apartment, even though the three men had no relatives here. He and his friends had fought together in Iraq and, later, in Korengal Valley, perhaps the most lethal area of Afghanistan. All three are now students and obviously find solace in each other's company. Few veterans have the option of continuing such proximal friendships with those with whom they lived and fought side by side. Yet like the veterans who set up household together, many others too search for community.

Although the immediacy of experience found in a writing workshop in an Afghanistan camp may be impossible to reproduce, two-year colleges and universities would contribute an immeasurable service to student-veterans by offering creative writing workshops, as well as introductory composition courses, customized for them. Academic institutions are in a unique position to prepare veterans for civilian career fields and to offer writing courses in which student-veterans can share, shape, and thus deflate some of the power from the moments that haunt. Veterans can begin to heal in the civilian world surrounded by a community of brothers and sisters.

Kelly Singleton Dalton, a helicopter pilot in the Second Gulf War and a second lieutenant in the Air Force, writes the following in her 2010 Georgetown University master's thesis, "From Combat to Composition: Meeting the Needs of Military Veterans through Postsecondary Writing Pedagogy": "For combat veterans suffering from psychological injuries such as post traumatic stress disorder, an understanding of writing as a way of making meaning, of shaping and reshaping experience, and of materializing realities in both the world and writer can be a positive source of self-healing" (4).

But it is much more than just the writing that heals—it is *being heard.* For veterans, it is knowing their pain is felt vicariously by those who possess the strength to listen, by those with courage enough to tilt a human ear toward their wartime stories and to risk being changed by the tremor in their voices. PTSD is, after all, a shared experience: when one family member is affected, the entire family suffers, and thus the community suffers. Maxine Hong Kingston, a longtime leader of veteran writing workshops, tells us that veterans' stories "are public acts of communication," requiring "mouth to ear transmission" (Kingston interview). Kingston and others are making a difference. Yet think of the former specialists, privates, and sergeants whose transition to both civilian life and academia might be made easier if veterans-only writing courses taught by instructors familiar with veterans' needs were widely available on college campuses.

The scientific research community concurs that writing about traumatic events provides emotional release and improves mental and physical health. James W. Pennebaker is a social psychologist and pioneer of writing therapy at the University of Texas at Austin. His findings reported in "Writing about Emotional Experiences as a Therapeutic Process" confirm the connection between writing or talking about emotional topics and the health of the body. Although Pennebaker was initially interested in whether people with powerful secrets might be more prone to health problems, he discovered that writing about those secrets, even if the writer destroyed the writing immediately afterward, had a positive effect on that person's health (Griffith 1). He determined that although the actual writing about traumatic events may be upsetting in the short term, the long-term psychological benefits of self-reflective, emotional writing include improved mood and overall sense of well-being (546). More surprising to Pennebaker were the physical effects of increased immune function and lowered heart rate, among other physiological improvements (540). As Tim O'Brien put it in the story "The Lives of the Dead," the act of turning his wartime trauma into narrative was one of "Tim trying to save Timmy's life with a story" (246). Tim was in effect healing not only his soul but his body as well.

Imagine this: You suddenly wake to find yourself a private in a military unit deployed to Helmand Province, Afghanistan. Until this moment you had been a civilian, a computer science major taking introductory courses at a community college. Now you run, bent low to the ground along a mud-brick wall, while a barrage of insurgents' bullets whiz inches above your Kevlar helmet. You wrap your fingers tighter around the buttstock of your M16. You say to yourself, "Just squeeze finger to trigger and shoot, dammit!" But then you remember that you have never aimed or fired a gun. You lack the tools to defend yourself.

This is how it feels for the vast majority of technically trained soldiers transitioning from war to the academic environment. It is also one of the most compelling reasons postsecondary institutions should offer introductory English and creative writing courses for veterans. "A student-veteran's expectations about language use have been shaped not only by military technologies and culture but also by the military's codified regulations, some of which address writing specifically" (Dalton 18). Soldiers are trained to write and speak in brief, concise (subject, verb, object) sentences that clarify, because ambiguous language could result in casualties on the battlefield. Army guidelines as outlined in *Effective Writing for Army Leaders* instruct soldiers, whether writing or speaking, to keep sentences brief, use words of three syllables or fewer, and use paragraphs that are no more than one inch deep (3-1). Written military communication emphasizes "brevity, clarity, and standardization of format," reducing writing "to an exercise in mathematical computations" (Dalton 22), one intended to minimize costly mistakes.

Academic and creative writing, on the other hand, require exploration, analysis, synthesis, interpretation, imagination. The skills used in both types of writing help us reimagine and re-create both the world around us and ourselves. The transition from the world of military language to working creatively with words requires a leap from the concise and concrete to a much more nuanced, rather than formulaic, use of words. Immersion in a language world so different from the military's is simply another way in which "student-veterans are, after all, negotiating ways of redefining themselves—both as students and civilian individuals" (25). Colleges and universities must help returning student-veterans become academic writers by raising their awareness of the differences between military and academic language use and by offering writing classes specifically designed to teach essay writing as a process of discovery and refinement through revision, a "process that is complex, organic, nuanced, creative, and singular to each writer" (24).

Compounding the challenges faced by veterans in adjusting to academic language and expectations are those moments of awkwardness that arise in a mixed class of civilian and veteran students. Curious about the veteran's experience in Afghanistan or Iraq, civilian students often ask inappropriate questions. Even the seemingly innocent "What was it like in Afghanistan/Iraq?" can unleash a torrent of emotions for the veteran. It is not unusual for a young student to innocently ask whether the veteran has ever killed. Imagine the shame involved in either response. Or consider this real-life example: In an introduction to literature class attended by a former student of mine, Mike, students had been assigned to read a short story in which one of the characters was a trained killer. During the class discussion a civilian student, knowing Mike had been in the military, asked what it felt like to be a trained killer. He wondered how the feelings of such a killer might differ from those of a murderer. You can only imagine the veteran's emotional response. Or, a professor makes a political comment opposing the US policy of sending troops to Iraq, the very war in which a veteran seated in the second row had served. As a soldier, he nearly lost his legs when his vehicle rolled over an IED. Although angered by the professor's comment, he remains silent.

Veterans may well experience other forms of dissonance in the classroom. The intensity of their life experiences creates a disconnect between them and the recent high school graduates occupying the surrounding desks. Veteran-students often miss the camaraderie of the military, deep friendships forged under extreme circumstances, and brotherhood or sisterhood in an organization, whether Army, Air Force, Marines, or Navy, in which its members share even a unique language of acronyms. Understandably, they feel like outsiders as they struggle to reinvent themselves as students. Once experts in a military specialty, they must begin a new life by calling upon the fortitude and discipline required in the past. It is no wonder soldier-students are put off by well-meaning civilian students who complain an assignment is "too hard" or that he or she couldn't complete homework because a math test had fallen on the same evening. In contrast, the veteran comes from an environment in which there are no excuses, and inattentiveness may cost a life. It is no wonder that veterans feel more willing to speak and write about their experiences in classes with brothers and sisters who have served in war.

In an interview with Bill Moyers, Maxine Hong Kingston states, "There's the coming home from war, being broken, feeling losses, but then there is a wholeness that takes place if the person [is] able to write their story, to write their poem, to have people hear them and listen and understand. Then they are changed again." It is not by forgetting the past that they are reborn, rather it is by mining the past for the gems that decorate and transform the present and future. As Kingston suggests, "People who care what we have to say surround us. They draw the stories out of us by their wanting to know" (*Veterans of War*, 2).

The creative writing prompts that appear in the following pages have proven useful to both the active-duty soldiers and the veterans I have taught throughout the years. I hope you also find them beneficial.

Thank you for the honor you have paid to our soldiers by being present to their words.

Christine Dumaine Leche

SELECTED BIBLIOGRAPHY

Ackerman, Robert, David DiRamio, and Regina L. Garza Mitchell. "Transitions: Combat Veterans as College Students." *New Directions for Student Services* 126 (Summer 2009): 5–14.

Branker, Cheryl. "Deserving Design: The New Generation of Student Veterans." *Journal of Postsecondary Education and Disability* 22, no. 1 (2009): 59–66.

Burnett, Sandra E., and John Segoria. "Collaboration for Military Transition Students from Combat to College: It Takes a Community." *Journal of Postsecondary Education and Disability* 22, no. 1 (2009): 53–58.

Dalton, Kelly Singleton. "From Combat to Composition: Meeting the Needs of Military Veterans through Postsecondary Writing Pedagogy." MA thesis, Georgetown University, 2010.

Department of the Army. *Effective Writing for Army Leaders*. Department of the Army Pamphlet 600-67. Washington, DC: Headquarters, Dept. of the Army, 1986. http://www.au.af.mil/au/awc/awcgate/army/p600_67.pdf.

Griffith, Vivé. "Writing to Heal: Research Shows Writing about Emotional Experiences Can Have Tangible Health Benefits." University of Texas at Austin, Office of Public Affairs. 10 January 2005. www.utexas.edu/features/2005/writing.

Kingston, Maxine Hong. Interview by Bill Moyers. Bill Moyers Journal, PBS, May 25, 2007, http://www.pbs.org/moyers/journal/05252007/transcript1.html.

———, ed. *Veterans of War, Veterans of Peace*. Kihei, Hawaii: Koa Books, 2006.

O'Brien, Tim. *The Things They Carried*. Boston: Houghton Mifflin, 1990.

Pennebaker, James W. "Writing about Emotional Experiences as a Therapeutic Process." *Psychological Science* 8, no. 3 (May 1997): 162–66.

Radford, Alexandria Walton. *Military Service Members and Veterans in Higher Education: What the New GI Bill May Mean for Postsecondary Institutions.* Washington, DC: American Council on Education, 2009.

Shay, Jonathan. *Achilles in Vietnam: Combat Trauma and the Undoing of Character.* New York: Scribner, 1994.

———. *Odysseus in America: Combat Trauma and the Trials of Homecoming.* New York: Scribner, 2002.

Shea, Kevin Peter. "The Effects of Combat Related Stress on Learning in an Academic Environment: A Qualitative Case Study." PhD diss., Kansas State University, 2010.

Writing Prompts

The prompts below are ones I have used with both active-duty soldiers and veterans in my creative writing and English classes. Following each piece I've included the title of a memoir from this collection to show how far from the original prompt memory can take us.

1. Write a scene in which three of the following appear: desert boots, M16, RPG (rocket-propelled grenade), Humvee, tank, helicopter, IED (improvised explosive device), cell phone, NVGs (night-vision goggles), computer, DVD, Great Voice, cigarette or cigar, photograph, wedding ring, wallet, money, foot locker. One object becomes central to your story, while the others remain incidental. ("On the Shoulders of Dead Men," SPC Andrew Stock)

2. Remember, creative writing is the opposite of thought. It is image making. Think of a moment of exhilaration you've experienced in the military, a moment when all of your senses were heightened and engaged. The type of experience you find tough to explain to an outsider, such as waking up in a sleeping bag in an open desert, a pale orange sun seeming to rise out of the earth 500 yards in front of you; stepping around the corner of a mud house to find the alley too quiet, too still; or lifting off the flight line in a Black Hawk at midnight. Use all five senses in describing the scene. Use at least three metaphors and/or similes. ("Field of Fire," SGT Jeffrey Lambert)

3. Imagine you are holding a camera. A camera captures exact images, but it cannot think, show feeling, summarize, etc. Write a dramatic memory. As you develop your narrative, practice moving the lens of your camera in close to capture minute details, which slows time down. Or set the lens for distance to speed time up. ("Routine Mission," SGT Kevin Zimmerman)

4. What is it that your relatives and friends won't understand about war when you return home? Write a monologue (use first person, "I," throughout) in which you re-create four brief scenes that attempt to show, through images that engage the senses, what perhaps cannot be fully explained: the meaning of war. Because war does not *mean*, but simply *is*, you will be creating pictures on the page, as if you are

showing photographs to a friend. Move abruptly from one scene to the next as you would from one photograph to the next. In other words, *show, don't tell*. ("Journal Entries," A1C Nicolas Gonzalez)

5. Write about a military event or other occurrence in your life about which you no longer feel guilty. Once you complete your narrative, take a second look at the first few paragraphs. How many paragraphs did it take you to reach the climax of your story? Would your story be stronger if you began in the middle of the action, in medias res, and you added the necessary background details contained in the opening paragraphs along the way? Revision is an indispensable part of the writing process. Your goal here is to grab the reader's attention in the first few sentences of your story. ("The Big Bang," Anonymous Male)

6. You are getting dressed, slipping an arm into your BDU or DCU shirt and thinking about what it means to be a soldier. Maybe you are standing in front of a mirror. Write your thoughts as you put on your BDU or DCU top, pants, army socks, desert boots—all symbols of commitment to your country. You might be thinking about what it means to serve, or if deployed, about what you may face today while wearing your uniform, or remembering a dangerous or difficult mission. You may feel pride, but what else? Are any of your thoughts contradictory? What does your uniform symbolize to your parents, your wife, husband, son, or daughter? Does it hold negative connotations for anyone close to you? Why? Don't try to cover all of the above. Go with your most powerful images. ("Deployment," SFC Billy Wallace)

7. Write a letter to the enemy. (no example)

8. Write about a time you got in trouble either with your command or on a mission. Your narrative should be a complete story, but not necessarily a long story. Include dialogue, description with lots of sensory detail, rising action, climax, falling action. Remember to *show* rather than *tell*. ("Meltdown," SGT Jarrell Robinson)

9. Plot involves conflict (man against man, nature, self, the environment, etc.). The antagonist might be a person but might also be a place or thing: the desert, an RPG or mortar, the insurgent's gun. What if the gun's eye is following you? What if it is following you and you are in a helicopter? What if you are flying the helicopter? Note how the tension increases with increased danger. Write about a situation in which the conflict is made more intense because several things are happening at once. ("Karbala, Iraq," SFC Billy Wallace; "Roses," SGT Josh Wyly)

10. Use one of the following places as a writing prompt: FOB (forward operating base), airfield, DFAC (dining facility), guard tower, Humvee hatch, tent, AAFES barbershop, hooch, chapel, front gate, or choose your own. ("B-Hut Blues," SFC Michael Bramlett)

11. Create a setting so alive it becomes a character. The setting is either with you or against you. You can also use this prompt to create a funny piece. A few places that lend themselves to humor downrange include the dining hall, AFFES barbershop, portable showers, Burger King, gym, DFAC. ("One More Day," SGT Jessie Evans)

12. Write about an incident to fit this formula: Desire + Danger = Drama. Remember, "desire" can mean anything from the desire to return to camp safely after a mission to the desire to locate an insurgent's weapons cache or the desire to talk to your wife on the phone. Crank up the tension so it influences the action and conversation throughout most of the story. You might also choose to write about some weird, funny, or silly incident. Even so, make tension part of your story. ("Another Day in Paradise," Benjamin Lowery)

13. Write about an abstract quality that you either left downrange or took with you from downrange to the civilian world. Some examples include trust, fear, hope, hate, love, anxiety, doubt, faith, desire, confidence, forgiveness. The challenge is to use the senses—sight, sound, touch, taste, smell—along with concrete detail to "show" how the event changed you. In other words, do not directly mention any of the above abstract words in your narrative (trust, fear, hope, etc.). Hint: Focus on a specific event that you make "happen again" on the page. ("I Would Rather Die in Afghanistan," SGT Elether Fareaux)

14. Choose a photograph and write the story it tells. Do not tell the story directly. For example, do not write, "I remember that day. I was about to leave for the day's mission in Helmand Province." Instead, as with all stories, immediately immerse the reader in conflict by using sensory detail, dialogue, exposition, and action to build tension and bring both your emotions, and thus the scene, to life. ("My Great Sadness," SGT Christopher Williams)

15. Using primarily dialogue, try to convince a younger sibling or friend to join or not join the military, to join the Marines instead of the Army (or Air Force), or to make the military a career. Use description to create location (park bench, pool hall, restaurant, living room, bar). How does the environment either fit or not fit the conversation? As the characters speak, show their meaningful expressions, physical movements, gestures, eye contact, etc., all the while

remembering that a character may act one way and think another. Remember, we are never *still* when we speak. Our body *speaks* as clearly as our words. ("Spring," SPC Chantal Ogaldez)

16. Write about an incident when you responded with anger or revenge, and you are glad you did. This incident can have to do with the military or not. ("The Big Bang," Anonymous Male)

17. Write about the day you left home for deployment. ("How Every Soldier Leaves," SGT Catherine Lorfils; "Deployment," SFC Billy Wallace)

18. Write a piece in which the main action is a conversation that takes place on either a cell phone or a field phone (remember the echo?). You are deployed to a faraway country—bad weather (wind, rain, or snow), worse food, a snoring roommate. Even while on the phone, you may be playing with a pencil, doodling, tapping your fingers on the table, watching someone across the room, pacing back and forth, listening to the guy next to you talk to his wife. How does your interaction with the environment mirror your conversation? ("Sat Phone Black Op," SGT Sean Moore)

19. Write from the point of view of your desert boots, M16, NVGs, flip-flops worn when showering downrange, Kevlar helmet, etc. (no example)

20. Write a conversation that takes place between you and a friend while visiting in your "hooch" (small sleeping quarters in a deployment zone). Your conversation will be trite since, just outside the plywood walls that define your space, other soldiers might be reading or resting in their cubicles. Maybe you and your friend are playing a video game or listening to music. Allow the video game to become a character in your story in the sense that it interrupts the human conversation. Why is the video game important? Why are you playing in the first place if the idea is to hang out and talk? The theme of your piece might be "Taking a Break from the War." (no example)

21. Write about a single contact with another human being in which the reader will see the pain or learn of the awareness that the event has caused you. Write this piece in third person, omniscient narrator (he, she). The narrator knows everything, can see your facial expressions, hear you breathe, knows what you think. Bring this scene to life. ("Coincidence," Anonymous Female)

22. Returning home from a deployment and reentering the civilian world of shopping malls, fast food restaurants, and grocery stores is a disconcerting experience for most. Driving a car, mowing the

grass, paying the bills, going to a movie theater—the most common actions and events can seem surreal. Hone in with microscopic description on one seemingly simple "civilian" task or daily occurrence. Rely heavily on the senses to convey your insecurity, awkwardness, even fear as you encounter the once familiar as a threat, challenge, etc. ("Protection," Marie Mulling)

23. Write a piece in which you compare and contrast the war games you played as a child with a real-life experience you had as a soldier. ("Sat Phone Black Op," SGT Sean Moore; "Bombed," SrA Michal Sakautzki)

24. You have just arrived home from a long deployment in Iraq or Afghanistan. Now it is time to unpack your duffle bag, both the real items and the memories they hold, as well as the emotional baggage with its invisible weight. Take the reader with you into the room back home where you unpack. Let us overhear your thoughts. ("Moving On," SGT Joseph Colvin)

25. Write about a time while deployed when you were affected by weather. Did weather play a factor in the outcome of a mission? A helicopter landing? Did weather affect your computer connection so you could not make contact with family in Montana? Use your imagination! ("Spring," SPC Chantal Ogaldez)

Abbreviations

AB Air base

ACOG Advanced combat optical gunsight

ACU Army Combat Uniform

AK-47 *Avtomat Kalashnikova 47* (automatic rifle)

ALICE All-purpose lightweight individual carrying equipment

ARCOM Army Commendation Medal

ASR Alternate supply route

AT Antitank ordnance

BDU Battle Dress Uniform

B-hut Semipermanent wooden structure used as a replacement for a tent

BOLO Be on the lookout

BSOPS Base operations

C-17, C-130 Military transport aircraft

C4 Plastic explosives

C&P Compensation and Pension

CASEVAC Casualty evacuation

COC Chain of command

CONEX Military shipping container

DAV Disabled American Veterans

DCU Desert Camouflage Uniform

DFAC Dining facility

EOD Explosive ordnance disposal

F-15, F-16 Fighters (US military aircraft designation)

FO Forward observer

FOB Forward operating base

GBU Guided Bomb Unit

GPS Global positioning system

HYEX Hydraulic excavator

IBA Interceptor Body Armor

IED Improvised explosive device

IOTV Improved outer tactical vest

IR Infrared reflective

ISAF International Security Assistance Force

JERRV (Joint Explosive Ordnance Disposal Rapid Response Vehicle)

JTAC Joint tactical air controller

KIA Killed in action

LN Local national

LZ Landing zone

M4, M16, M40 Military assault rifles

M240B, M249B Machine guns

MEPS Military entrance processing

MK19 40mm grenade launcher

MOS Military Occupational Specialty

MP Military police

MPI Military police investigator

MRE Meals ready-to-eat (field rations)

NCOIC Noncommissioned officer in charge

NOD Night observation device

NVG Night-vision goggles

OIC Officer in charge

PAX Passenger terminal

PL Platoon leader

PMCS Preventive maintenance checks and services

PT Physical training

PTSD Post-Traumatic Stress Disorder

QRF Quick reaction force

R&R Rest and relaxation

REDCON Readiness condition

RER Round-expenditure report

RP Rally point

RPG Rocket-propelled grenade

RPK Kalashnikov light machine gun

RTO Radio telephone operator

S2 Battalion or brigade intelligence staff officer

SAW Squad automatic weapon

SF Security Forces

SGLI Servicemembers' Group Life Insurance

SITREP Situation report

SMAW Shoulder-launched multi-purpose assault weapon

SOP Standard operating procedure

TACC Tactical air command center

TBI Traumatic brain injury

TIC Troops in contact

TOC Tactical operations center

UXO Unexploded ordnance

VA Veterans Administration

XM4 Experimental shoulder-fired rocket launcher ("bunker buster")

ZOS Zone of separation

Zulu Greenwich Mean Time

MILITARY RANKS

A1C Airman first class

AFSC Airman second class

CO Commanding officer

COL Colonel

CPL Corporal

CSM Command sergeant major

LCDR Lieutenant commander

1LT First lieutenant

LTC Lieutenant colonel

NCO Noncommissioned officer

PFC Private first class

PV2 Private second class

PVT Private

SFC Sergeant first class

SGT Sergeant

1SG First sergeant

SPC Specialist

SrA Senior airman

SSG Staff sergeant

TSGT Technical sergeant